Vita & Virginia

First published in the United Kingdom in 2018 by
National Trust Books
43 Great Ormond Street
London
WC1N 3HZ

An imprint of Pavilion Books Company Ltd

ISBN 978-1-91135-838-1

A CIP catalogue record for this book is available from the
British Library.

10 9 8 7 6 5 4 3 2 1

Reproduction by Mission Productions Ltd, Hong Kong
Printed and bound by GPS Group, Slovenia
This book can be ordered direct from the publisher at
www.pavilionbooks.com

CONTENTS

⋮ Vita's Writing Room ⋮

Vita Sackville-West kept two photographs on the desk of her writing room, high up in the Elizabethan tower at Sissinghurst Castle in Kent. One was of her husband, the writer and diplomat Harold Nicolson. The other was of the novelist Virginia Woolf. The brief physical passion Vita and Virginia shared was already over before Vita and Harold bought Sissinghurst in 1930, but Virginia told a friend, just months before her death, that apart from her husband Leonard and her sister Vanessa, Vita was the only person she really loved.

The writing room was, and is still, a shrine to Vita's complicated, colourful life – a room where salvaged treasures from her aristocratic past jostle souvenirs of her foreign adventures, and the tools of her trades as both a gardener and a writer. On the battered oak writing table itself, under the misty grandeur of a tapestry evoking her ancestral home of Knole, is an everyday jumble of pens and paper clips, spectacles and soil samples; a reproduction of a famous painting of the Brontë sisters; a small vase of flowers on a block of lapis lazuli; the bound memoirs of a seventeenth-century heiress known as 'La Grande Mademoiselle'; her amber cigarette holder; a set of Post Office scales; and a tiny calendar with pictures of Alsatian dogs. A small cupboard on the corner of the table once held a souvenir of her Spanish grandmother Pepita – one of her dancing shoes.

Vita was often alone in this very private domain. Her sons entered it only half a dozen times in all their years at Sissinghurst. But, surrounded by echoes of those she valued, she would not have been lonely.

Everything in the room had meaning for Vita, from the photo of her beloved Alsatian Rollo to the turquoise ceramic clam shells she had bought on her travels in the East with Harold. (She gave one to Virginia to use as an ashtray.) From the blue glass given to her by her adored, difficult mother to the Chinese crystal rabbits that made their way into her most successful novel. From the box in which she kept

Vita's desk, in her workroom on the first floor of the tower at Sissinghurst, featured a framed photograph of Virginia Woolf as well as one of her husband Harold Nicolson.

Above and opposite: Vita at her desk. She always dreamt of living alone in a tower with her books, and at Sissinghurst she fell in love with the 'bewitched and rosy fountain' shooting towards the sky.

press cuttings about Virginia's books, to the small picture of the earlier Sackville lady who inherited Knole, as Vita herself longed to have done. Virginia Woolf always relished the aristocratic aspect of Vita: 'Snob as I am, I trace her passions 500 years back, and they become romantic to me, like old yellow wine.'

When Vita and Harold began the task of making the ruined Sissinghurst habitable, one of the first things they did was to knock through the wall from the tower room into the adjoining turret. Today, the octagonal turret room is lined with books from floor to ceiling. Books on plants and gardening, annotated by Harold in pencil and by Vita in coloured pens. Books on earlier writers, or earlier adventurous aristocrats, from Dorothy Wordsworth to Lady Caroline Lamb. Books on the occult or spiritual subjects, like Sir James Frazer's classic *The Golden Bough*. And books on sexuality and gender identity, a hot topic of the 1920s and '30s, such as Havelock Ellis's *Psychology of Sex* and Edward Carpenter's *The Intermediate Sex*,

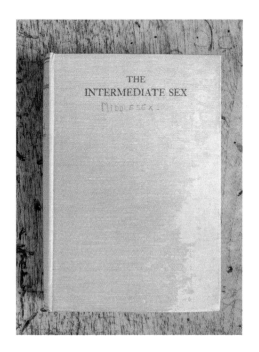

The books Vita kept in her tower at Sissinghurst ranged in subject from gardening to geography, and travel to sexuality.

on the cover of which Vita printed the word 'Middlesex'.

Books written by Harold are in the writing room itself. A first copy of his biography of Tennyson, published in 1923, is inscribed as being presented to Vita Sackville-West 'by her lover Harold Nicolson'. They had then been married almost a decade, and would be married for four decades more, their love unimpeded (except on one notable occasion) by the fact that both had affairs with their own sex.

Beneath the many bookshelves of the turret room is a rough wooden cupboard. In it, after Vita's death, her son Nigel Nicolson found a battered leather Gladstone bag. Earlier, Vita had written to Virginia a laughing apology for sending her letter in an old envelope. She had lost, she said, the small stout key which 'unlocks not only my reputation but my stationery'. For in the cupboard, in the Gladstone bag, Vita had left the memoir she wrote of her frantic affair with Violet Trefusis – the one affair which, in the years immediately before she met Virginia, had almost overthrown her marriage.

Vita's relationship with Virginia, which began shortly after, was of a different calibre – a relationship in which both Harold Nicolson and Virginia's husband Leonard were supportive presences. The bond that endured between those two women was predominantly, though not exclusively, one of the heart, and of the mind.

Vita reverenced Virginia's writing. 'I don't know whether to be dejected or encouraged when I read the works of Virginia Woolf. Dejected because I shall never be able to write like that, or encouraged because somebody can.' Virginia was sometimes less complimentary about Vita's 'sleepwalking servant girl novels'.

Previous pages: The view from Sissinghurst's tower shows part of the Yew Walk and the Rose Garden, with the South Cottage where Vita and Harold slept.

'Why she writes, which she does with complete competency and a pen of brass, is a puzzle to me. If I were she, I should merely stride, with 11 Elk hounds behind me, through my ancestral woods.'

Today, indeed, Vita is remembered chiefly for the garden she created at Sissinghurst, rather than for the many words she herself spun, while Virginia Woolf appears on any list of modern literary greats. Yet in the late 1920s Vita Sackville-West was the inspiration for one of Virginia Woolf's most enchanting novels.

Orlando celebrates the Vita of the ancestors and the elkhounds, but it celebrates, too, Vita's venturesomeness, her adventures into sexual identity. Together, as well as separately, Vita and Virginia explored the question of what it meant to be a woman. And the story of the closeness they shared gives them both another claim on our attention today.

Everything in Vita's workroom had a meaning for her, like the blue ceramics she began collecting when in Persia with Harold.

PART I

1882–1922
Moments of Being

CHAPTER 1

⋮ Vita, 1892–1913 ⋮

Vita (Victoria Mary) was born in 1892 at Knole in Kent, the granddaughter of Lionel Sackville-West, second Baron Sackville. Her mother was Lord Sackville's adored, but illegitimate, daughter Victoria, one of five offspring of Lionel's liaison with a Spanish dancer, Pepita. Vita's father was Lord Sackville's nephew and heir: Vita's parents were first cousins. The house had come into the possession of the Sackville family in the sixteenth century, granted by Elizabeth I to a Sackville kinsman. Vita's tragedy, as she saw it, was that as a girl she could never inherit the place that played such an important role in her imagination.

The main block meanders, in Vita's word, from the late fifteenth to the early seventeenth century, on every turret a heraldic Sackville leopard. But the most astonishing thing about Knole is its vast four-acre sprawl – more like a town than a house, Virginia Woolf would say. Vita herself wrote that after a lifetime's familiarity with the house, she still found herself pausing to work out the best route from one room to another. Three long galleries are packed with important paintings; a 'King's Bedroom' contains an entire set of furniture made from beaten silver. Vita found that 'shockingly vulgar' ('Charles Sackville cannot have known when he had enough of a good thing'), though thousands of visitors disagree. She preferred the Chapel of the Archbishops, in what is now the private part of the house, where is kept the carved Calvary bequeathed to a Sackville by Mary Queen of Scots; this

Above: A bookplate from Vita's library at Sissinghurst. Her mother had different bookplates drawn for each of her most precious books.

Opposite: The great Jacobean staircase at Knole features the heraldic Sackville leopards.

Deer still roam Knole's 1000-acre park. It was the excellent hunting and healthy air that led Henry VIII to covet the place.

is where Vita herself, following in the footsteps of her parents, would eventually be married.

In medieval times Knole had been a palace of the archbishops of Canterbury, reft from Thomas Cranmer by Henry VIII, who coveted its healthful situation and fine stag hunting. Vita remembered an encounter with a stag who wandered, curious but unafraid, into the Great Hall. Even today, though Knole's great park sits within the very town of Sevenoaks, deer camp out beside the walls of the house.

An early chatelaine was the diarist Lady Anne Clifford, wife to the Jacobean owner with whom she was forever at enmity. Her diaries are full of her keeping to her chamber, with 'a sorrowful and heavy heart'. Knole became a prison to her. Vita could not have felt more differently. As a little girl she used to roam the galleries with a candle, alone and unafraid. She wrote with all the warmth of memory about the light gleaming on gilded furniture and old mirrors. A carved or painted face might start out of the gloom or the figures on a tapestry move. The ancient house was full of noises … but she was never frightened at Knole, she wrote. 'I loved it; and took it for granted that Knole loved me.'

Even as a child she would browse among the family archives, picking out strange plums, from the menu for a Stuart banquet ('Roast venison, in blood', whole pig, boiled teats, almond pudding) to the fact that one Sackville ancestor had been granted, in 1648, 'the East Coast of America'. These were the details – the colours, the light through stained glass, the glow of firelight on old wood – that would years later illumine *Orlando*. Knole was a whole world, a small village in itself, and the child Vita was as fascinated to watch the mangle being turned in the laundry, or the gamekeeper skinning a deer, as she was to observe the luxuriance and artificiality of her beautiful, extravagant mother's dresses, or the diamond monogram on the shell of her pet tortoise. These were the kind of details

Vita's grandmother Pepita Durán was a dancer before her liaison with the future Baron Sackville. She was noted for her long black hair and tiny feet.

that would later make their way into Vita's own bestselling novel, *The Edwardians*.

Vita wrote a book, too, about her grandmother, 'Pepita'. Josefa Durán – to give her legal name, rather than the stage one by which she became internationally known – was a Spanish dancer who, by the time Vita's mother Victoria was born in 1862, had already for ten years been conducting an affair with the English diplomat Lionel Sackville-West. Pepita's father was a barber, her mother a former washerwoman. (Vita, in the memoir her son Nigel Nicolson published as *Portrait of a Marriage*, would describe her grandmother, more romantically, as the illegitimate daughter of a gypsy and a Spanish duke, and indeed, Nigel Nicolson noted, the combination of 'the gipsy and the grandee' did represent the two sides of her character.)

There was no question of Lionel marrying Pepita. She was still legally married to her former dancing teacher, and their daughter Victoria was registered as *'fille de père inconnu'*, daughter of an unknown father. But it was an established ménage

– the children never knew they were illegitimate – and Lionel set up his mistress and their five children in a villa in south-west France, where Pepita styled herself the Comtesse West. The strange idyll ended abruptly in 1871 with Pepita's death. Lionel the diplomat was then stationed in Buenos Aires, an unreachable distance away. For two years the children were left in the charge of neighbours, then the girls were sent to board at French convents. It was 1880 before he was able to sweep his controversial French-speaking family over to England, to be received with guarded welcome by the Sackville-West family.

Victoria, however, did not stay in England for long. Lionel had been appointed British Minister to Washington in the United States, and the eighteen-year-old Victoria (after some tactful enquiries as to whether, though illegitimate, she would be happily received) accompanied him as his hostess. It sounds like a daunting challenge for so inexperienced a girl, but in fact her beauty and charm took Washington by storm. She would later list for Vita the 25 proposals of marriage she claimed to have received from diplomats or men of title. One of them came from President Arthur himself. Five years after they had arrived, the American papers were speculating on why 'the most beautiful woman in diplomatic circles' was still unmarried. But in 1888 a piece of careless speaking – a letter to a trickster, breaking the rules of diplomatic neutrality by giving his views of the forthcoming presidential election – put an end to Lionel's diplomatic career. His elder brother's death had transformed him into Lord Sackville, so it was to Knole that the family returned.

Since the new Lord Sackville's children by Pepita were illegitimate, his title would eventually devolve on his nephew – another Lionel, confusingly. He was one of the first visitors to the new regime at Knole. He was fascinated by the glamorous Victoria, five years older than he, and soon they planned to marry. From the moment she accepted him, after an initial reluctance, their courtship was conducted with a note of rampant sensuality. They were married in the chapel at Knole on 17 June 1890; the Prince of Wales, the future Edward VII, had sent an engagement gift of a diamond and pearl brooch. As Victoria would say: *'Quel roman est ma vie!'* ('What a story my life is!') In the early days of their marriage, their passion for each other continued unabated. They made love – and Victoria's diary recorded each occasion – in the bath, the park, on a fur rug and the library sofa. In the summer of 1891 she knew that she was pregnant.

Vita's birth was horrific – a hundred times worse, so Victoria recorded, than anything she had expected. (She begged for chloroform, but her husband couldn't

The famous beauty of Victoria, Vita's mother, drew many admirers throughout her life.

Vita with her mother in 1900, when a motor car was very much a novelty. This was the first to be installed in Knole's stables.

get the bottle open.) She was, however, immediately besotted with her new baby. Vita was Victoria's pet – showered with dolls, sharing her mother's bed when her husband was away – but shunned when she failed to conform to Victoria's standards of femininity. Vita's feelings about her mother would remain conflicted – looking back, at one moment she would comment that she much preferred her father, and was frightened of her mother's quick temper; at the next, that her mother, though the most incomprehensible, was also the most charming person on earth 'whom I adore'.

The local dancing teacher would complain that the tomboy Vita was rough. Vita herself would later say that the normal child 'thoroughly enjoys being unkind to something'. She remembered tying visiting children to a tree, thrashing their legs with nettles and stuffing their noses with putty. She made a great ideal, she wrote, of being 'as like a boy as possible'. In her memoir she would recall herself as 'plain, lean; dark, unsociable, unattractive – horribly unattractive! – rough, and secret.'

Despite all of this, Vita had a great ally in her grandfather, whose 'Sackville family failing of unsociability' meant he shunned visitors to the house, and left young Vita to show off its glories. He was, she recalled, 'very old, and queer, and silent', but he liked children. Theirs was a reciprocal alliance – her grandfather kept in his desk a drawer marked as Vita's, where he would secrete treats of fruit for her after dinner every night. Her life was an isolated one, but far from unhappy, despite the fact that, by the turn of the century, her parents were getting on very badly.

Vita remained an only child – her mother Victoria had wanted no more pregnancies. Thwarted by a lack of sex in his home, Lionel turned (to his wife's relief) to a lover, Lady Constance Hatch. At Victoria's insistence, she and Lionel kept up appearances as husband and wife, and continued to attend functions together.

Victoria herself found other interests with Sir John Murray Scott, the fabulously wealthy, 25-stone bachelor fifteen years older than she, who had inherited Hertford House and the staggering collection of artworks now known as the Wallace Collection. The Sackville-Wests, by contrast, were permanently short of money. Sir John – 'Seery' – bought Victoria a Mayfair house; her husband Lionel accepted the friendship gratefully along with Seery's continued subsidies to Knole.

Seery treated Vita as a daughter. His gift of a cricket set became one of the eight-year-old's most treasured possessions. She and Victoria (and, indeed, Lionel) stayed with him in his huge Paris apartment on the rue Lafitte, or at the shooting lodge he took yearly in the Scottish Highlands.

At the age of thirteen Vita began attending day classes at a small school off London's Park Lane, and it was in these years that she developed an intimacy with two young women whose passion for her – a passion she reciprocated – was to help shape her future.

These two girls were Rosamund Grosvenor and Violet Keppel (later Trefusis). Rosamund – four years older than Vita, and a relative of the Duke of Westminster – had been a family friend who once shared Vita's lessons at Knole. Lovely yet passive, she fell under the spell of the more dynamic Vita, whose attraction towards her was wholly physical. Violet Keppel was a more complicated kettle of fish: Vita's son Nigel Nicolson writes that to read Violet's childhood letters after Rosamund's is 'like handling rockets after sparklers'.

The daughter of Alice Keppel, mistress to Edward VII, and her husband, a son of the Earl of Albemarle, Violet was two years younger than Vita. Deeply precocious and passionate, she was committed to the idea that each individual had one great love in them. Vita was to be hers.

They had everything in common, from a glamorous family connection to an addiction to books and a strong link to France. Having first met at a tea party, their paths continued to cross, notably in Italy, in the spring of 1908, where – according to Vita – Violet 'told me she loved me'. At sixteen, Vita was nearly six feet tall – and now officially the 'Honourable' Vita Sackville-West (Vita's grandfather had died that autumn, so her father had inherited the barony).

Sir John Lavery's 1919 portrait of Violet Trefusis clearly shows the allure that would come close to wrecking Vita's marriage.

Or was she? Her mother's brother Henry was all too aware that it was only the bar of illegitimacy preventing him – a son rather than a mere nephew – from inheriting the Sackville title. He pushed ahead with the court case through which he had long sought to claim back the title. To win, he would have had to prove not only that his mother Pepita had married old Lord Sackville but also that she had never been married to her Spanish dancing teacher. When, early in 1910, the case finally reached the courts (not to mention the papers) it was decided that he had failed to do this.

When Vita's parents won the lawsuit over the Sackville inheritance, the townspeople of Sevenoaks gave them a triumphal welcome home.

Victoria – to protect her husband's title and her own position – had, ironically, been forced publicly to protest her own illegitimacy. When Vita and her parents returned home to Knole in triumph, the men of the local fire brigade celebrated their victory by unhitching the horses and themselves pulled their carriage up to the house. The small family were newly established in their tenure of Knole – although Vita was aware that as a girl, the entailed estate could never be her own. Her mother 'made all the capital she could out of the house; to hear her talk about it you would have thought she had built it'. By contrast, Vita noted her father's inarticulate devotion to the house – and perhaps her own sick passion. But her life was expected to lie elsewhere.

In 1910 Vita was painted by Philip de László, and went to stay with Rosamund at Fiesole above Florence, where she was once again courted by the Italian Marchese Pucci, who on an earlier visit had fallen in love with her.

Vita at eighteen was no longer the priggish teenager, 'unmanageably and lankily tall'. She had blossomed, though she still described her coming out as a

Vita's eighteenth birthday was marked by a portrait from the society painter Philip de László. Later in life she disliked it as being 'too smart'.

Smallhythe Place was home to the actress Ellen Terry. She lent her presence to a Shakespeare masque in which Vita also took part.

Vita wore the robes Ellen Terry had once worn in the role of Portia in *The Merchant of Venice*.

'distasteful and unsuccessful process'. She was studious and had been writing since childhood: tales of adventure and poetry; plays and historical novels, many of them about her own family; a diary. On 29 June 1910, at a London dinner party, she met the young diplomat Harold Nicolson. She asked him down to Knole, to watch a Shakespeare masque that was being performed in the park by a mixture of amateurs and professionals, including her Kentish neighbour from Smallhythe, the great ageing actress Ellen Terry, and Mrs Winston Churchill.

Vita continued to invite Harold to Knole, he continued to accept. But when a summer 'flu which threatened pneumonia saw her mother take her south to a villa near Monte Carlo for six months, it was Violet Keppel who gave her the more emotional send-off. When they returned home in the spring of 1911 – Vita to accompany her father to the coronation of King George V – she continued the round of debutante parties.

Vita had a car which, unconventionally, she drove herself; she also had a bear cub she took for walks on a chain in Knole park. She had a strong physical attraction to Rosamund Grosvenor as well as an affection for Harold Nicolson, who had returned home sick from his post at the British Embassy in Madrid. Harold was the son of a successful career diplomat (and his mother's sister was married to the former Indian Viceroy, Lord Dufferin), but he had no money to recommend him to Vita's parents as a great match. The only child of Knole might have hoped for something better; nor did Harold – flirting with a young male friend – seem any more committed than Vita.

In January 1912, Seery, for so long a father figure to Vita, died. The day after she heard the news she attended a great ball at Hatfield House and there, tearing button after button off his evening gloves, Harold asked her to marry him. She begged him to wait; her mother insisted there should not yet be an official engagement (and that their correspondence should contain no such endearments as 'darling'). As Harold set off for his next posting in Constantinople, Vita continued her life of country house visits, of the loathed parties, of proposals.

But Vita wrote every few days to Harold, and he to her. It was only to her diary that she admitted she was desperately unhappy, now sure she did not love him. Weeks later, however, she was telling her mother he was all her life. Rosamund was often at Knole, and since no engagement had been announced Vita continued to receive attention from other, very eligible, men. Her suitors included Lord Granby, son of the Duke of Rutland, and Lord Lascelles, who could have made her chatelaine of the fabulous Harewood House and who, when she turned him down, would marry King George's daughter Princess Mary instead.

> *Vita would write in her memoir that 'men didn't attract me, that I didn't think of them in what is called "that way". Women did.'*

That spring she went to Florence with Rosamund; she told Harold she was not ready yet. If they married in the autumn 'it will end – after all, I'm only twenty!' She had not definitely turned down Lord Lascelles when Harold returned home on leave in the summer. But on the last weekend of September, before returning to his post, Harold kissed her as they walked through the showrooms of Knole and called her his wife. It was the kind of positive gesture she required of her lovers; 'I love him.'

But that was very far from the end of the story. As Harold returned to Constantinople, Vita and Rosamund returned to Florence, and Rosamund felt able to tell Vita, 'Men may come and men may go, but I go on for ever.' Vita would

Both Vita's suitor Harold Nicolson and Rosamund Grosvenor accompanied Vita and her father to court when in 1913 his family contested the legacy Seery left to Victoria.

write in her memoir that 'men didn't attract me, that I didn't think of them in what is called "that way". Women did.' And it was Violet Keppel, not Harold, of whom Rosamund was chiefly jealous. At Christmas, Vita told her diary 'I can't, I can't give up everything for him'; in May she sent Harold a telegram calling off the engagement. When he wired back asking whether he was to take it seriously, she wired back, no. As Rosamund became engaged to a naval officer, Violet too became engaged, to Lord Gerald Wellesley.

But in the first half of 1913 – in the midst of a London season that saw Vita lunching at the Ritz with Rodin, with John Singer Sargent, with Mrs Astor – the Sackville family had another problem on their minds. Seery had left Vita's mother a generous amount of money in his will – and a stunning collection of furniture, which she promptly sold. (Victoria's new admirers were the American millionaires J.P. Morgan and William Waldorf Astor.) But now Seery's family contested the will, claiming undue influence had been brought. When the case came to court in June it galvanised both the press and polite society.

Vita, with Harold (once more back on leave) and Rosamund, accompanied her parents to court to witness Lady Sackville's triumphant performance. Vita said it reawoke her adoration of her mother – it was only later she realised how distressing it must have been for her father. 'Kidlet' – to use the pet name the court heard Seery had given Vita – was called upon to give evidence. One of the accusations was that her mother had been seen surreptitiously going through Seery's private papers two years before, presumably looking for any codicil to the will. Vita was able to prove she had been unwell that day, and her mother had been with her. The case collapsed – as it was always going to do – but Vita had felt like a coconut in a coconut shy. In the relief that followed the case, however, she told Harold she would marry him in the autumn.

William Strang's 1918 portrait of Vita, *Lady with a Red Hat*, was in Harold Nicolson's opinion a true reflection of Vita. It shows how far she was moving away from the Edwardian society beauty de László had portrayed.

CHAPTER 2
⋮ Virginia, 1882–1913 ⋮

In *A Sketch of the Past*, a partial memoir she wrote in 1939, Virginia Woolf mockingly described her own origins. Adeline Virginia Stephen, as she identified herself by her full name, was born on 25 January 1882, the second daughter of Leslie and Julia Prinsep Stephen, and descended, she joked, from a great many people; some famous, others not. Her parents were well-to-do, though not rich, and altogether she could congratulate herself on being born 'into a very communicative, literate, letter-writing, visiting, articulate, late nineteenth-century world.'

Her father Leslie Stephen – himself the son of a distinguished colonial administrator, academic and anti-slavery campaigner – was a friend to men like Henry James, William Makepeace Thackeray and Robert Louis Stevenson (the authors, respectively, of *Vanity Fair* and *Treasure Island*). Originally ordained a clergyman, Leslie Stephen renounced his faith and turned to literature, as the author of groundbreaking essays such as *An Agnostic's Apology* and *Freethinking and Plainspeaking*. Three years after Virginia's birth he would also become the founding editor of that enduring institution, the *Dictionary of National Biography*.

Virginia's mother Julia was Leslie Stephen's second wife. His first marriage, to Thackeray's daughter Minny, had ended with her death in pregnancy. The

Virginia's father Leslie Stephen was a noted Victorian man of letters, essayist and thinker.

Photographed in 1902, when she was about 20, the young Virginia Stephen had the lambent beauty of her mother Julia, a model for a number of Pre-Raphaelite painters.

Virginia's mother Julia also frequently modelled for her aunt, the pioneering photographer Julia Margaret Cameron.

beautiful Anglo-Indian Julia was herself a distraught widow, her adored barrister husband Herbert Duckworth having died early. Like Leslie Stephen, she came from a notable family whose connections would help to shape Virginia's world. Julia's own mother had been one of seven famous Pattle sisters whose connections (in the Little Holland House set that formed around Julia's aunt Sara Prinsep) ranged from Millais to du Maurier, from Tennyson to Watts and the Pre-Raphaelites. Another of Julia's Pattle aunts was the photographer Julia Margaret Cameron. Virginia's mother had been a model for Cameron, and for Watts and Burne-Jones too.

Vanessa (left) and Virginia (right) flanking their half-sister Stella Duckworth, who became something of a mother figure to them before her own early death.

The family's Anglo-Indian origins were spiced by the memory of a James Pattle of Calcutta who had once married the daughter of the Chevalier de l'Etang, page and perhaps lover to Marie Antoinette. But Virginia's family could boast a strong line of pioneering and reforming women as well as literary and successful men. The infinitely complex web of family connections was perhaps the precursor of what would come to be identified as the Bloomsbury Group. Many of the members, indeed, were the same.

When Leslie Stephen became a widower in 1875, Julia was already the mother of three Duckworth children aged ten or under – George, Stella and Gerald. She had known the Stephens – they moved in the same elevated and artistic circles – and now, by coincidence, she was living next door in Hyde Park Gate. She and Leslie were married on 26 March 1878. Their elder daughter Vanessa was born in 1879 and their elder son Thoby sixteen months later. A fourth child, Adrian, would follow Virginia in 1883.

The family home at 13 (later renumbered as 22) Hyde Park Gate, off Kensington Road and near the new museums, was a large house, cluttered in the Victorian fashion, of which Virginia would write as if with the observant but incurious gaze of childhood. She and her siblings moved 'like ships in an immense

Vanessa playing cricket with Adrian Stephen, the youngest of the four siblings.

ocean … happily encircled by firelight', while the adult world of 'legs and skirts' left them untouched. Much of her mother's time was taken up with good works, both amid the poor and among her own extended family, and with the demands of the exigent Leslie Stephen. Virginia complained that she rarely saw her mother alone. Later she would write, in *A Room of One's Own*, of her own efforts to strangle the long-suffering, self-abnegating 'Angel in the House' that her mother's life represented. Had she not killed the Angel, 'she would have killed me.'

It was a world of daily walks in Kensington Gardens where Virginia sailed her toy ship on the Round Pond, of shared stories the children made up, of instructive talks with her father, after their mother had taught her daughters their first lessons. Of, as Virginia later wrote, 'plain duties' and 'appropriate pleasures'. But she did not wait until adulthood to record her childhood – from February 1891, when Virginia had just turned nine, the Stephen children produced the breathlessly handwritten *Hyde Park Gate News*, in imitation of their favourite *Tit-Bits* magazine.

Talland House, overlooking St Ives Bay, was for twelve years the beloved summer home of the Stephen family. Memories of holidays there would later colour Virginia's novel *To the Lighthouse*.

It was also a world of summers by the sea. Leslie Stephen had found Talland House, overlooking St Ives Bay, on a walking holiday in Cornwall in 1881, and first took his family to visit the following year – the year of Virginia's birth. The small fishing town was already beginning to attract the attention of tourists, and of artists. Leslie Stephen called it a 'pocket-paradise', of soft sea breezes and a garden full of hidden corners to delight a child, bursting with 'grapes and strawberries and peaches', with a path leading down to a sheltered sandy beach. There, for the next dozen years, the family would spend the long summer months from June to October. The early memory of the sound of the waves and the sight of the wind making the window blind swell and billow like a sail was one that would recur through Virginia's adult fiction. Leslie Stephen wrote of their life there as 'a long series of scenes of intense domestic happiness.'

That, of course, was only one side of the coin. As the boys were sent away to school Thoby was recorded as suffering from bouts of 'delirium', and what could have been a suicide attempt. There was a cousin damaged by a blow to the head

The closeness of Vanessa (pictured) and Virginia did not preclude rivalry. Virginia could resent her sister's 'supremacy' – her supposed greater femininity.

– he would end his young life in an asylum – who became obsessed with the now adult and increasingly beautiful Stella Duckworth. And there was Laura, Leslie Stephen's daughter by his first wife Minny, 'a vacant-eyed girl whose idiocy was becoming ever more obvious', as Virginia later recalled. It is impossible for us to know from exactly what Laura was suffering, but by the early 1890s she was residing in an 'idiot asylum' in Redhill.

Laura's existence was not the only challenging memory Virginia described in *A Sketch of the Past*. There was a slab outside the dining room of Talland House for standing dishes upon, and once 'when I was very small', her half-brother Gerald Duckworth, twelve years older than she, lifted her onto it and, as she sat there, 'began to explore my body'. She could remember, she wrote, the feel of his hand going under her clothes, lower and lower. She remembered how she hoped that he would stop, how she stiffened and wriggled as his hand approached her private parts. In 1941, very shortly before her suicide, she wrote to a friend that this incident still made her 'shiver with shame'.

Other traumas were ahead. In early March 1895 the thirteen-year-old Virginia described her mother as 'very weak' after the 'flu. Her health never recovered. The weakness turned to rheumatic fever, and before the first week of May was out, Julia was dead. Virginia – like the other children – was brought into her mother's room so that Julia could say goodbye to the daughter whose eccentricities had made her the family's 'little Goat' – and brought in, too, to see her mother's dead body. Virginia would remember that kissing it was 'like kissing cold iron'. She was afraid 'of not feeling enough'.

Leslie Stephen had already decided to give up Talland Lodge, since a hotel was to be built, blocking the view. It was the end of the St Ives idyll. Instead, the family went to summer at Dimbola Lodge at Freshwater on the Isle of Wight, Julia Margaret Cameron's family home, with her photographs of Julia Stephen on the walls. Virginia wrote that the place was 'choked with too luxuriant feelings'.

That Virginia Woolf was 'mad' has become axiomatic, her madness paradoxically seen as the reverse side of her genius.

Many years later Virginia would make a comedy, *Freshwater*, out of a 'summer afternoon world' of the house's heyday, replete with great bowls of strawberries and the beauty of the Pattle sisters, with the glamour of guests like Tennyson and Ellen Terry. But at this time she was 'half-insane with shyness and nervousness', suffering 'intermittent waves of very strong emotion' – often, of rage. Beyond even her own loss, she was reacting against her father's histrionics, agonies and the outward parade of mourning demanded by the time.

Even before Julia's death there had been mention of Virginia's 'difficulties'. Raging mentally 'at father, at George', reading endlessly, she was for two years unable to write. That Virginia Woolf was 'mad' has become axiomatic, her madness paradoxically seen as the reverse side of her genius. Sometimes, her symptoms sound more like what later eras would call depression. For the rest of her life, the web of external circumstance and internal predisposition – of social pressure, as distinct from biochemistry, hormonal disturbance or what seems now like hamfisted medical treatment – cannot be unpicked. But the family felt it necessary to consult a doctor, who prescribed a complete absence of lessons and four hours of outdoor exercise a day.

Her life with the family continued – a family holiday to Brighton the following spring, and to Hindhead the following summer, where Stella became engaged to the family friend and trainee solicitor Jack Hills. He was a welcome influence in Vanessa and Virginia's lives; the love he shared with Stella was a spectacle she described as an ideal for her – 'glowing, red, clear, intense'. The preparations for the spring wedding were happy, the April marriage day one of white roses and lace dresses. The couple set off on a brief honeymoon, but on their return Stella began to experience health problems – a chill, an inflammation of the stomach – complicated by the first stages of pregnancy.

In June Virginia herself fell ill with a rheumatic fever and was being nursed in Stella's house. (Leslie Stephen had consented to his stepdaughter's marriage only on condition that the young couple moved in next door to him.) On the night of 14 July it was Stella who was sitting up with a Virginia tormented by 'the fidgets' – the family word for nerves. But abruptly Stella's own condition worsened and, despite an emergency operation, in a few hours she was dead. It was an extraordinary parade of losses and challenges for Virginia, who had not yet reached her sixteenth birthday. Small wonder that in her diary of 1 January 1898 she was urging herself to 'have courage and plod on'.

Just as Stella had previously been expected to take on her mother's role, so the eighteen-year-old Vanessa was now expected to take on Stella's. It was 'Nessa' who was forced to take responsibility for balancing the household books, facing her father's unreasonable and unrestrained cries that they would be ruined. But Virginia too would carry her own legacy of frustration and anger at her father's 'blind, animal, savage' rages.

As the Stephen sisters reached marriageable age, their eldest half-brother George (a conventional Victorian, Virginia said, while she and her full siblings were intellectual moderns) embarked on a campaign to launch them into polite society. Their father Leslie was now in retreat, failing in health and deaf. Both sisters found the experience excruciating – 'the Greek slave years', Virginia called them. Both – Vanessa with her dawning artistic talent and Virginia with her writing – were 'always battling for that which was being interfered with, muffled up, snatched away.' But George's pressure, to put it no higher, did not end there.

His advances were less directly sexual than Gerald's had been, a decade before. They were, however something Virginia's nephew and biographer Quentin Bell would describe as a 'mawkish incestuous sexuality', which in his opinion left Virginia permanently seized in a 'posture of frozen and defensive panic'. When George came to Virginia's room at night, flinging himself onto her bed, 'kissing and cuddling and otherwise embracing me' it could be argued that his demands – his abuse – were emotional rather than physical: he had, Virginia later agreed with Vanessa, a 'half-insane' quality. She also said that: 'He sent me mad.'

It has been argued that the fact both sisters remained on reasonable terms with George, and that Virginia's husband Leonard would always describe him as an

extremely kind man, suggests a degree of confusion as to just how inappropriate his behaviour really was. It has been suggested even that when, in 1921 and 1922, Virginia described his behaviour in readings to the Bloomsbury Memoir Club she was making a consciously literary construct. Vanessa, however, seems to have shared Virginia's view of George's behaviour.

Nonetheless, as with the earlier disturbances in the family, there was no actual breach. While Vanessa was accepted into the prestigious Royal Academy Schools to continue her studies in art, Virginia found the windows opened by her own studies of Latin and Greek, as well as her experiments in writing. They would be pushed further open by acquaintance with her brother Thoby's Cambridge friends (several of whom already had family connections with the Stephens' wide circle).

Thoby Stephen, the eldest, was a dominant figure, known as 'the Goth' to his friends.

Thoby entered Trinity College, Cambridge in 1899, where he immediately formed a group with several people who would later feature as members of the Bloomsbury set: Clive Bell, Lytton Strachey, Leonard Woolf. There was, at the time, no sign that the last-named would be Virginia's future husband, although Leonard later wrote that it was virtually impossible for any man not to fall in love with both the beautiful Stephen sisters, whose formidable qualities shone through their demure Victorian surface.

The explorations these young men made together – in the Shakespeare Society, in their own play-reading group, the Midnight Society, and through the exclusive, secretive 'Apostles' or 'Conversazione Society', whose members past or present also included the artist and critic Roger Fry, the journalist Desmond MacCarthy, the economist John Maynard Keynes and E.M. Forster – would prove important in the years ahead. They were all, as Leonard later put it, profoundly committed to the rejection of a 'religious and moral code of cant or hypocrisy'. At a time of immense social and intellectual change they were conscious of being the vanguard of 'the builders of a new society which should be free, rational, civilised …' These

Virginia's first Bloomsbury address was 46 Gordon Square. She, Vanessa and their brothers moved there after their father's death. Today a blue plaque marks the house.

were the creeds that would build the group identified as 'Bloomsbury'. But before Bloomsbury could be born another death in the Stephen family was necessary.

It was the death of Leslie Stephen on 22 February 1904 (followed, in the summer, by George Duckworth's society wedding to the Earl of Carnarvon's daughter) that would prompt his children to remove from Hyde Park Gate to the cheaper Bloomsbury, then seen as beyond the fringes of polite London. Leslie Stephen had been four years dying from bowel cancer, and the wait was agonising for all. Now, on every level, their father's death marked a profound change for the Stephen sisters.

Years later Virginia would write that only his death made her writer's life possible. Had he lived to old age, 'His life would have entirely ended mine … No writing, no books; – inconceivable.' But her feelings about the man who had in his earlier, easier years encouraged her were intensely complex, in thrall to him even as she sought to separate herself and even, in the years ahead, use *Orlando* to challenge his idea of biography.

46 Gordon Square was the first of a series of residences which would give name to the 'Bloomsbury' set.

If Virginia's feelings after her father's death were a dangerous cocktail of grief, regret and guilt, Vanessa's were less ambiguous. That spring she swept the family up on a European grand tour to enjoy the art of the great cities: Venice, Florence, Paris. But her siblings' open pleasure left Virginia – as after her mother's death – feeling profoundly isolated. The day after their return to England in May, she collapsed.

Feeling a profound anger against Vanessa, against whom she launched a long diatribe, she was sent to stay outside London with Violet Dickinson, a philanthropic and independent friend of the family who had become something of a mother figure to her. Violet hired three nurses but Virginia nonetheless attempted to throw herself out of a window, albeit one on the ground floor. She was suffering from hallucinations, hearing the birds singing in Greek and the King, Edward VII, 'using the foulest possible language' in the azaleas. (Perhaps the effects of the hypnotic drugs she would have been given must be taken into account.) Virginia herself attributed the voices to overeating, and sought to starve herself out of hearing them. Later in life, her weight would continue to fluctuate wildly. By September she was well enough to start to rejoin the family on occasion, and by November to move into the new home Vanessa had been making.

The five-storey house, in a square developed in the 1820s but since fallen somewhat from its original respectability, 46 Gordon Square was the first of a

Vanessa painted by Duncan Grant, a friend from the early days of
Bloomsbury and briefly her lover, despite her marriage to Clive Bell.

series of closely interconnected residences that would give name as well as locale to the 'Bloomsbury' set. From the 'rich red gloom' of the Victorian age into the lighter, less constrained world of the new … An air of 'cleanliness and emptiness' in which even the objects from the old house – 'Watts pictures, Dutch cabinets, blue china' – looked different, Virginia recalled. The house only reflected the ideas of the inhabitants. 'Everything was going to be new; everything was going to be different. Everything was on trial.'

It was a household of four siblings clinging together: Thoby, 'the Goth', as his Cambridge friends called him, whose position as eldest male made him the natural leader; Adrian the nervous youngest; Vanessa, now studying at the Slade; and Virginia in her top room, all too conscious of the need to make money, not least to pay for her own recent medical bills. She was writing reviews as well as more personal essays and, in the summer of 1906, the first 40 pages of what might more than a decade later become her first novel, *The Voyage Out*.

Virginia was always intensely conscious of the relationship of Vanessa's painting to her own writer's art, and would see her own diary as a 'sketch book'. The events of their life had forced the sisters into a 'very close conspiracy', a 'private nucleus' – but they had also cast Vanessa in the role of caretaker. She was the responsible one, a position guaranteed to foster a certain amount of resentment on both sides. In later years Virginia would write to Vanessa that perhaps they two had the same pair of eyes, only seeing through different spectacles – but she would write, too, of 'Nessa's overwhelming supremacy'.

Virginia was also developing close relationships, tinged with eroticism, with a number of older women outside her immediate family, able to offer the protective tenderness she would later demand of Vita. 'Put some affection into your letters', she would beg Violet Dickinson. 'My food is affection!' Describing their relationship as a 'romantic friendship', Virginia would present Violet with 'Friendship's Gallery', a fantastical personal tribute typed up in violet ink. It would foreshadow her tribute to Vita – *Orlando* – prescient, too, in that the gift would mark a change in the relationship.

In many ways, however, it was a male group who first found their meeting place in Gordon Square. The Thursday evenings of conversation and cocoa Thoby set up were mostly arranged for his Cambridge circle, with his sisters comparatively silent participants in what were not at first very lively sessions. Virginia declared that 'women are my line, not these inanimate creatures'. Duncan Grant remembered that for some years Virginia's manner towards men would be 'aloof and a little fierce'.

Grant was a new addition to Bloomsbury, Lytton Strachey's cousin and sometime lover, and a former lover of Adrian Stephen. A number of these young men found their first sexual experience with other men, though not all of them would remain homosexual, or exclusively so. The handful of proposals of marriage that the young Virginia Stephen would receive came from this Cambridge group – but not yet from Leonard Woolf, who came to Gordon Square for a farewell dinner before departing for Ceylon (Sri Lanka) and a seven-year stint in the colonial service.

There was still more trouble in store for the Stephen family. Vanessa set up the Friday Club to discuss art and arrange exhibitions as the four Stephen siblings made a return visit to St Ives; as Vanessa rejected a proposal from Thoby's Cambridge friend Clive Bell, saying the warm liking she felt for him was not enough for marriage, the siblings also, in the autumn of 1906, set off on a trip to Greece. On their return, both Thoby and Vanessa became ill with typhoid – from which, on 20 November, Thoby died. Violet Dickinson had accompanied the Stephens and was herself too ill to be told of Thoby's death, so that Virginia was forced to write her fictitious – and convincingly detailed – accounts of his progress towards recovery. His ghost would later haunt her fiction, notably as the absent Percival in *The Waves*.

In the shock of the news, Vanessa accepted a fresh proposal from Clive Bell. They married on 7 of February 1907, at St Pancras registry office. Inevitably, Vanessa's reaction – and her happy physicality, as she and Clive received guests in bed together – set her apart from Virginia, who felt she had lost not only a brother but a sister. Virginia and Adrian were to move together to 29 Fitzroy Square (west of Tottenham Court Road and into what would now be called Fitzrovia rather than Bloomsbury). But Virginia would find little support in Adrian – the baby of the family – later in life a founder of British psychoanalysis, but now still to find his path. He was depressive and, so Virginia felt, disdainful of her.

The birth of Vanessa's first child, Julian, early in 1908, heightened the difficulty. With Nessa absorbed in her baby, Virginia was drawing closer to Vanessa's husband Clive. She had once dismissed him as a 'parakeet', but in fact she would come to value his literary judgement as well as his sensuality: 'I warm my hands at these red-hot-coal-men.' Her rapprochement sparked Clive into seeking a full-blown affair, and though Virginia never succumbed, it could not but colour her relationship with a suspicious Vanessa.

As before, however, the family bonds held even under so many stresses; Virginia now seemed to be drawing closer to Lytton Strachey (already a central figure in

Bloomsbury and beginning to make his name as a critic, though far still from his innovative theory of biography). It was starting to seem imperative within the family that Virginia should marry – she complained of the pressure and Lytton, despite his homosexuality, seemed a likely candidate.

Lytton did propose to Virginia one evening and was accepted – or, in the course of a muddled conversation, it seemed that way – but was enormously relieved when the next day Virginia changed her mind and refused. (In the years ahead the young painter Dora Carrington, in love and cohabiting with Lytton, would marry Ralph Partridge – the object of Lytton's love – in order to maintain their three-way relationship and keep Partridge as a friend for Strachey. It is not for nothing that Dorothy Parker would describe the Bloomsbury set as living in squares, loving in triangles and painting in circles.)

Lytton Strachey was already writing to Leonard Woolf in Ceylon suggesting he should take on the role: 'you would be great enough and you'd have the immense advantage of physical desire.' Leonard responded to Lytton's first proxy advance by saying that if Lytton really thought Virginia would accept him, he'd take the next boat home. But for the moment, while Lytton and Virginia stayed close all their lives, Leonard remained in Ceylon. Virginia, however, was, Lytton said, 'young, wild, inquisitive, discontented, and longing to be in love.'

> *Virginia was, Lytton Strachey said, 'young, wild, inquisitive, discontented, and longing to be in love.'*

Virginia herself would later declare, 'I was rather adventurous, for those days; that is we were sexually very free,' adding, however, 'but I was always sexually cowardly … My terror of real life has always kept me in a nunnery.' The bold talking, the rambling around London, the sitting up all night with young men seemed brave at the time, and was certainly unconventional for an Edwardian young lady but was actually, she said in retrospect, 'rather petty'. Lytton Strachey would say of her that she was her name – Virginia, virgin – but another of the Bloomsbury group, Sydney Waterlow, would say that Vanessa was the icy one, interested only in art; Virginia was more emotional and interested in life.

Virginia was however already contemplating, like other intellectual women of the early twentieth century, whether it was possible to have both marriage and a writing career. She told Violet Dickinson that she saw her future as 'a virgin, an Aunt, an authoress'. (The analogy of writing a book and having a child was

Virginia (far left) and five other pranksters perpetrating the notorious 'Dreadnought Hoax', pretending to be the retinue of the Emperor of Abyssinia in order to board a naval warship.

common currency within her family.) The last years of her spinsterhood would see her engage in new adventures.

In 1905 she'd begun two years of voluntary teaching with Morley College, an evening institute for working men and women, sited under the stage of the Old Vic theatre. In 1910 she undertook another form of social involvement as she engaged briefly with the suffrage cause, addressing envelopes and attending a couple of mass meetings. Yet in a year when suffragettes were embarking on projects like November's 'Black Friday' demonstration in Parliament Square – which saw six hours of street fighting and 200 arrests – Virginia's involvement can only be called half-hearted. Perhaps it was another attempt to kill the 'Angel in the House'; her mother had disapproved of female suffrage. Later in life her book *Three Guineas* would display Virginia's profound commitment to feminism, but also her instinctive mistrust of the very kind of male organisation – Parliament – that the suffragettes sought to join.

More characteristic, perhaps, was another venture of 1910, the so-called 'Dreadnought Hoax'. In February Virginia, Adrian, and Duncan Grant joined in a scheme set up by the notorious poet and prankster Horace de Vere Cole. In costume and wearing dark make-up, the group pretended to be the retinue of the Emperor of Abyssinia in order to get on board HMS *Dreadnought*. Their way paved in advance by a letter to the First Lord of the Admiralty, they were welcomed aboard by a naval band and red carpet, despite their babble of 'Bunga-Bunga', Latin and pidgin English and Virginia's male disguise. Cole subsequently leaked the story to the press, but the widespread reports made no mention of Virginia's name. The more responsible among Virginia's immediate family and friends were horrified – her more distant naval relatives doubly so. But perhaps what seems now like a distasteful prank seemed to Virginia like a gesture of subversion towards military authority – a piece of the playfulness later seen in *Orlando*. Her judgement may have been off-kilter, since that summer she slipped once again into a depression, forced to endure a six-week 'rest cure' – drinking milk and, she complained, being shut up in dark rooms. (She was convinced Vanessa, who had imposed the cure on

Leonard Woolf had been one of Thoby Stephen's Cambridge friends. But when they married, Virginia joked that she was marrying 'a penniless Jew'.

her, was a 'dark devil' involved in a 'great conspiracy' against her.) But then again, Bloomsbury at this time was all about making subversive gestures.

In contrast to the Dreadnought Hoax, the 'Manet and the Post-Impressionists' exhibition organised by Roger Fry at the end of 1910 seems now like the most respectable of artistic endeavours. But at the time, the more conservative elements in society and in the press regarded it in just the same light, as an example of mental imbalance that could threaten the very stability of the British race. It can only have caused further outrage when in the new year the Stephen sisters were photographed scantily dressed as characters from a Gauguin painting, 'incredibly beautiful and very naked', at the Post-Impressionist Ball, held to raise money for the suffrage cause.

Fry was a new addition to the ever-shifting Bloomsbury circle – a former Cambridge 'Apostle' already in his forties, and with a wife trapped in lasting mental illness. When, towards the end of her own life, Virginia was asked to write his biography, she would single out the Post-Impressionist exhibition as a key moment in his life – and, indeed, of that of Bloomsbury. It was the year when she saw a new, 'Georgian' writing break away from the old 'Edwardian' style, the year when she got to know E.M. Forster (another new introduction to Bloomsbury but already famous as the author of *A Room With a View*). The year when, she would later say, 'human character changed'.

Suffrage, shocking art, sexual freedom … When Vanessa and Clive Bell set off for Turkey in the spring of 1911, Roger Fry went too, and when Vanessa suffered a miscarriage and breakdown it was Roger who cared for her. By the time Virginia came out on the Orient Express to bring Vanessa home, Nessa and Roger were moving towards a passionate affair. It was, however, supposed to be a secret from Virginia and her irresponsible tongue – 'she's really too dangerous', Vanessa said.

Virginia herself was beginning to accept the general opinion that she should marry. She would soon be 30. 'To be 29 and unmarried – to be a failure – childless – insane too, no writer.' She turned down a proposal from another old Cambridge acquaintance of Thoby's. She had a close new friendship with the Cambridge poet Rupert Brooke, who she had known in childhood. He was now a romantic figure, leader of the group Virginia christened the 'Neo-Pagans', devoted as they were to liberalism and outdoor living. When she visited Rupert Brooke at Grantchester, outside Cambridge, they went swimming naked in Byron's Pool. When they (with Maynard Keynes and Lytton Strachey) went to join the group of Neo-Pagans camping on Dartmoor, Leonard Woolf, home on leave from Ceylon, came too.

Leonard now had his eyes firmly fixed on Virginia. He found that Bloomsbury had moved on in the time he had been away – as had the Stephen girls. He relished 'a circle in which complete freedom of thought and speech was extended to both sexes.' 'I have always been greatly attracted by the undiluted female mind, as well as by the female body', he wrote later in his autobiography.

In the autumn Virginia invited him to spend a weekend at Asheham, the country house she and Vanessa had rented. She and Adrian were to move out of 29 Fitzroy Square, where the lease was up, and into the larger 38 Brunswick Square.

Maynard Keynes and Duncan Grant were to share the ground floor, Adrian to have the first floor and Virginia the second – and the top floor was offered to Leonard Woolf.

In January 1912 Leonard attempted to propose to Virginia and, when the meeting was interrupted, explained his feelings by letter. He was, he declared, jealous, cruel, lustful, a liar 'and probably worse still.' He had told himself over and over he would never marry anyone because of those defects. Virginia, by contrast, 'may be vain, an egoist, untruthful, as you say', but these were nothing compared to her other qualities. Magnificence, intelligence, wit, beauty, directness – and after all, he said, they liked one another, liked the same kind of things …

Virginia was not ready to give up her freedom, she wanted to 'go on as before'. But Vanessa wrote to Leonard assuring him that 'You're the only person who I know whom I can imagine as her husband.'

Virginia had been drawn to Rupert Brooke, whose mental health, however, was as fragile as her own. She was attracted also to the French artist Jacques Raverat, who was to marry someone else. But there was much about Leonard too that drew her attention.

The fourth of nine children, his father had been a successful barrister and QC whose death left his family in distress. His grandfather had been a London tailor and Leonard felt alien to the 'intellectual aristocracy' to which the Stephens belonged. He said that: 'although I and my father before me belonged to the professional middle class, we had only recently struggled up into it from the stratum of Jewish shopkeepers.' Virginia would write to her friends that she was marrying 'a penniless Jew'. Though his Classics scholarship to Cambridge introduced him to the largely homosexual circle whence sprung so many of the Bloomsbury set, Leonard had lived with a mistress in Ceylon.

His years with the Colonial Service had given him an experience different to her own, and perhaps the more attractive for it.

Leonard suffered from a nervous tremor in the hands which made him socially inhibited. But his years with the Colonial Service – uncongenial though he had found it to be 'governing natives, inventing ploughs, shooting tigers', as Virginia put it – had given him an experience different to her own, and perhaps the more attractive for it. (She would later write of how she valued Vita's 'hand on all the ropes'.)

On 1 May she sent Leonard a letter, exploring her conflicted feelings.
'I say to myself. Anyhow, you'll be quite happy with him: and he will give you
companionship, children, and a busy life.' But then she swore she was not prepared
to look upon marriage as a profession.

The very strength of his desire could sometimes make her angry ... 'is it the
sexual side of it that comes between us? As I told you brutally the other day, I feel
no physical attraction in you. There are moments – when you kissed me the other
day was one – when I feel no more than a rock.'

She had some feeling for him which was 'permanent, and growing', but she
could still pass from hot to cold in a flash. She was half afraid of herself. 'I feel
I must give you everything; and that if I can't, well, marriage would only be
second-best for you as well as for me.'

The stakes were getting very high. 'We ask a great deal of life, don't we?',
she asked rhetorically. But through the spring they saw each other almost
every day: walks in Regent's Park; concerts; attending the inquiry into the
sinking of the *Titanic*. She finally accepted him after a day on the river at
Maidenhead.

They were married on 10 August 1912, at St Pancras Registry Office, where
Vanessa and Clive Bell had married. Vanessa and George Duckworth were the
witnesses, though Leonard's mother did not attend.

• • •

The first years of Virginia's marriage are all about questions. She had said yes when
a previous suitor asked whether she wanted 'to have children and love in
the normal way'. But something went wrong on her honeymoon with Leonard.
They spent their wedding night at Asheham, followed by a few days in Somerset
and a continental tour. The days were spent sightseeing, reading, writing.
Virginia was working on what would become *The Voyage Out* while Leonard
finished a book of his own, *The Village in the Jungle*, and began work on *The
Wise Virgins*. Virginia wrote to a friend that she had lost her virginity and found
'the climax immensely exaggerated', but even that limited enthusiasm may have
overstated the case.

Leonard had always desired a marriage, he wrote, in which he could be 'mind
to mind and soul to soul'. But physical desire was part of the package. Now,
however, as the writer Gerald Brenan heard later: 'When on their honeymoon he

tried to make love to her, she had got into such a violent state of excitement that he had had to stop, knowing as he did that these states were a prelude to her attacks of madness.'

Vanessa, consulted 'on the subject of the Goat's coldness', said Virginia 'never had understood or sympathised with sexual passion in men'. Vanessa's son Quentin believed that youthful experiences with the Duckworths confirmed her disposition 'to shrink from the crudities of sex'. By the time the honeymoon couple reached Venice, Virginia was suffering from her tell-tale headaches and refusing to eat. By the time they got back to England Leonard was already, as he would write in his autobiography, 'troubled and apprehensive'. They moved into rooms in the Dickensian surroundings of Clifford's Inn off Fleet Street.

October 1912 saw a Second Post-Impressionist Exhibition at the Grafton Galleries – featuring Cézanne, Picasso, Matisse and new British artists like Stanley Spencer and Wyndham Lewis, along with Duncan Grant and Vanessa Bell. The following year Roger Fry also opened the Omega Workshops, with himself, Vanessa and Duncan Grant as the directors, and George Bernard Shaw among the investors. Everyday objects were individually created, anonymously, by all or any of the artists in their circle and sold with the distinctive Omega signature.

At 33 Fitzroy Square the ground floor was divided into two showrooms, with studios and workshops above. Society clients included Ottoline Morrell and Lady Cunard. But when Vita went with the Sitwell brothers to see Roger Fry's furniture at the Omega Workshop she found it 'horrible'. The Nicolsons' society was still that of the great hostesses – the 'Edwardian relics' as Vita would later think of them.

> *The Nicolsons' society was still that of the great hostesses – the 'Edwardian relics' as Vita would later think of them.*

Leonard Woolf had been secretary to the Second Post-Impressionist Exhibition, but his own work would be increasingly in the sphere of socialist politics: working with Sidney and Beatrice Webb for the Fabian Society; for the League of Nations Society; for the Ceylon independence movement; becoming secretary of the Advisory Committee to the Labour Party on International Questions; taking a leading part in the founding of the 1917 Club. Novels (and later autobiography) apart, he had a staggering output of volumes with titles like *Co-operation and the Future of Industry*, or *International Government*.

The decorative creations of the Omega Workshops set up by Roger Fry came to epitomise the Bloomsbury style. The celebrated the colour and freedom seen in the work of the Post-Impressionists.

Virginia too was pushing herself to finish *The Voyage Out* as 1912 turned to 1913. The heroine's journey to South America is very much a rite of passage, but one that does not end happily: perhaps a recognition both of the changes in Virginia's life, and of her fears.

She returned to the nursing home in Twickenham where she had stayed in 1910, and seemed a little better. But she now began expressing anger towards Leonard. (Vanessa would later write that she had taken against all men.) As she left the nursing home in August to celebrate their wedding anniversary she became delusional, convinced everyone was laughing at her and refusing to eat.

Back in London Virginia found Leonard's drug case and swallowed 100 grams of veronal. Leonard called Geoffrey Keynes, a doctor as well as Maynard's brother, who brought a stomach pump, and worked through the night. In the early hours of the morning she almost died. She was sent to George Duckworth's home Dalingridge Place in Sussex to convalesce, with Leonard and four nurses who had to use force to make her eat or rest. By November – much heavier, from all the meals and milk that featured heavily in the cure – she returned to Asheham, though still with a nurse in her room at night. But the possibility of a recurrence of the madness would forever be a third party in her marriage to Leonard.

CHAPTER 3

⋮ Two marriages, 1913–21 ⋮

Vita Sackville-West and Harold Nicolson were married on 1 October 1913, in the chapel at Knole. Vita was resplendent in silk encrusted with gold, but the night before she had cried for a solid hour at the thought of leaving Knole. The chapel held only 26 guests, but four duchesses were among the hundreds who attended the reception. The next day, from the garden of the house lent to them for their honeymoon, Vita told her diary 'I never dreamt of such happiness.' Harold, she wrote to her mother, had been 'full of tact and gentleness and consideration'.

Therein lay the rub, maybe … Vita would later, in her 1920 memoir, write that his lovemaking was 'like a sunny harbour' to her – that she never knew the physical passion with him that she had with Rosamund Grosvenor. But as the young couple set out for Constantinople, where Harold was still third secretary at the embassy – via Florence, and via Cairo, where Lord Kitchener entertained them – Vita was able to convince herself that her life was complete.

Their wooden Turkish house in Constantinople was charming; her husband was perfect – 'so gay, so funny, so clever, *so young.*' Within weeks of her marriage, however, Vita became pregnant, and the following summer the couple returned to Knole for her confinement. She returned also to a Rosamund who had now broken her engagement. So too had Violet (whose fiancé Gerald Wellesley would marry the heiress Dorothy, 'Dottie', who would later become another of Vita's friends and lovers).

● ● ●

For Virginia Woolf, 1914 saw a slow recovery. In February the doctors wrote that the time had come to rely on Virginia's 'self-control'; in May Leonard wrote that she was still 'a little up and down'.

Vita and Harold were married in the chapel at Knole. Vita described it as small, but 'very much bejewelled', and smouldering with colour.

Virginia and Leonard Woolf, at the time of their engagement. Despite her initial reservations, theirs would prove to be an enduring partnership.

The conflict in Virginia's own mind must have been more immediate to her than the war that broke out that summer. Later, of course, the First World War would shape many of her books – but in 1914, after all, the assumption was that the fighting would be over by Christmas. The Bloomsbury set were never going to join in with the jingoistic fervour that swept the rest of the country. Lytton Strachey called it 'muddle and futility'; Clive Bell published a pamphlet calling for negotiations to be opened with Germany.

The war bit harder – in April 1915, Rupert Brooke died of blood poisoning on his way to Gallipoli – and positions began to crystallise. Clive Bell was among those who found refuge working on the farm at Garsington Manor, where visitors from Bloomsbury had often enjoyed the luxurious hospitality of society hostess and literary patron Lady Ottoline Morrell. Lytton, Duncan and David 'Bunny' Garnett declared themselves conscientious objectors and faced trial; Ottoline's lover, the philosopher Bertrand Russell, actually served a term in Brixton gaol.

Vanessa Bell, whose affair with Roger Fry had now ended, was now beginning one with Duncan Grant (once the lover of her brother Adrian), though without detriment to Duncan's interest in Bunny Garnett. In the autumn of 1916 they all three, with Vanessa's two young sons, moved into Charleston farmhouse in Sussex where Duncan and Bunny could avoid conscription by working on the land. Leonard Woolf was pronounced unfit to fight because of the tremor in his hands, though as the need for troops grew ever greater he had to face not one but two medical boards. One of his brothers was killed and another wounded, and his political work would from this point tend towards the prevention of future war.

Lytton Strachey, Virginia Woolf and philosopher Goldsworthy Lowes Dickinson, photographed by Lady Ottoline Morrell. Her home Garsington Manor was a favourite country refuge for the Bloomsbury set.

Meanwhile, however, October 1914 had also seen the publication of Leonard's *The Wise Virgins*, about a young Jewish man's coming of age and rejection of his suburban mother and siblings. It also detailed the young man's rejection of the chilly bluestocking to whom he was initially drawn, in favour of a more sensual type. Leonard's family were sure enough of its autobiographical content to be deeply offended; the reaction of Vanessa and Adrian was much the same. Virginia read it on 31 January 1915; in February, coincidentally or otherwise, she once again suffered a breakdown.

At the end of March she returned to Twickenham for a week, but left to join Leonard at their new home in Richmond, Hogarth House, half of an imposing red-brick Georgian building with a long garden and spacious shabby rooms. But by the end of April she was, Leonard wrote, worse than he had ever seen her before. She had not slept in two or three days, and had attacked one of her nurses, Vanessa told Clive. In May Vanessa thought an asylum 'might be inevitable', though Leonard, having inspected a couple, said he would do anything rather than send her to one of those 'dreadful gloomy places'.

Hogarth House in Richmond, where the Woolfs lived for almost ten years, gave its name to their publishing imprint, the Hogarth Press.

Leonard's role in Virginia's treatment has been much debated over the years. Even Vanessa, while grateful for his care of Virginia, felt he was sometimes overly controlling. Vanessa's daughter Angelica would describe him as 'a vigilant and observant mastiff', made of some material hard as the rock of ages and retaining always 'something of the administrator of the Hambantota District in Ceylon.' When Leonard went away, a playful contract required Virginia, *Mandril Sarcophagus Felicissima*' – their nicknames for each other were Mandril and Mongoose – to swear that she would rest for a full half hour after lunch, be in bed by 10.25 every night, have her breakfast in bed and drink a *whole* glass of milk in the morning.

Virginia would later write, 'Of course Leonard puts a drag on, & I must be very cautious, like a child, not to make too much noise playing'. On another occasion, she wrote of how she felt Leonard was always 'castrating my joys'. Time and again, through the course of their marriage, she would cast Leonard as the protective but also repressive parent. Was it fair? And, is it fair of subsequent generations to blame him for an attitude that was supported by the medical opinion of the time? Virginia would tell Vanessa that she had married Leonard because he was 'absolutely dependable & like a rock which was what she badly wanted.'

There have certainly been questions about the way in which – without medical advice – he would administer or withhold her medication. But the rules both of their society and their marriage cast Leonard as the rational one, the legislator. It has been speculated, however, that her bouts of illness were in some way a reaction against that restrictive framework.

Rather than any sliding scale of – as she put it – 'melancholy', Leonard drew a clear line between a sane Virginia with 'a kind of mental balance', and a sick one in whom he saw 'violent emotional instability and oscillation … a refusal to admit or accept facts in the outside world'. When Virginia was well, he said, she recognised herself that she had been mad, and he described her as suffering both manic and depressive states.

Those around Virginia traced a malign connection between her writing and her breakdowns. The pious Jean Thomas, who ran the nursing home in Twickenham where Virginia on several occasions spent time, voiced the conventional view when she wrote to Violet Dickinson that it was 'the novel which has broken her up'. Vanessa agreed, echoing popular feeling with the suggestion that she had 'worn her brains out'. One of the doctors Leonard consulted – T.B. Hyslop, a believer in eugenics – felt that the 'new breed of intellectual women', and notably writers, were 'deleterious to the virility of the race'.

But other, romantic, ideas have long perceived madness and genius as different sides of the same coin. Virginia herself would make a connection. She certainly valued the times of retreat from the world she used to stave off bouts of what she called madness. In *On Being Ill*, she wrote of how the invalid, 'irresponsible and disinterested', is able for the first time to look at the sky. Of how, when the lights of health go down, 'undiscovered countries' open to the view – the 'great confessional' where truths are blurted out which health conceals.

But she seems also in a sense to have valued the 'madness' itself. 'As an experience, madness is terrific I can assure you, and not to be sniffed at' she wrote years later, 'in its lava I still find most of the things I write about. It shoots out of one everything shaped, final, not in mere driblets, as sanity does.' Did Vita, too, trace any connection between her wild side and her writing? But would she, unlike Virginia, always pull back from the brink?

• • •

At the time the First World War had broken out, Vita too had been preoccupied with the strife raging within the Sackville family. Her baby was born a few days later, and her plan to name him Benedict – rather than his grandfather's name of Lionel – sent her mother into an irrational frenzy. Christened Lionel Benedict, the boy would always be known as Ben, but a shaken Vita lamented that her mother was ready 'to fling me aside like an old glove.'

Several of the young men Vita knew would be killed in the war; her father would be at Gallipoli. Her husband Harold however was seconded to the Foreign Office, while Vita undertook part-time work at the Red Cross enquiry office. As they moved out of Knole and into 182 Ebury Street, Belgravia, Vita was uncharacteristically sociable and happy. She and Harold were a nice young couple to invite to dinner, she wrote later – 'Oh God, the horror of it.' She had, she said, been 'thoroughly tamed'. By December 1914 she was pregnant again. She knew, as she described it, 'absolute happiness', guilty only at thinking of other people's misery in a time of war. But the following November, with her second baby weeks overdue,

Vita photographed with her sons Ben (left) and Nigel (right) in the years she knew Virginia Woolf, who however complained she was 'a little cold & offhand' with her boys.

Vita and Harold created their first garden at Long Barn. The pattern of living they established there foreshadowed their later life at Sissinghurst.

she went into labour only for the doctors to have to remove a dead child. She was devastated – 'that little white velvet coffin with that little still thing inside … I can't help minding and I always shall.'

That spring she and Harold had purchased a house for sale in a village a mere two miles from Knole. The ancient Long Barn – legend has it that the printer William Caxton was born there – was on the way to becoming their first real home. Harold began to plan a garden and Vita, with enthusiasm but as yet no knowledge, began to plant. They dismantled an old barn to make a new wing with a fifty-foot drawing room and, eventually, would set up a separate cottage in which their children and the nanny could sleep, establishing, in other words, the pattern they would later follow at Sissinghurst.

Vita's parents were now getting on extremely badly. Lionel had embarked on an enduring affair with Mrs Olive Rubens and had adapted the old laundry at Knole as accommodation for her and her husband. Victoria bought three large houses in Brighton for her own refuge and was planning to turn them into one under the advice of Edwin Lutyens – the great architect having been the latest to fall under her spell. (He would shortly be succeeded by the soap tycoon Lord Leverhulme.)

In 1916 Vita fell pregnant again, and her second son, Nigel, was born without problem in January 1917. That October her first book, *Poems of West and East*, was published to favourable notices. But at the end of the month Harold told her he suspected he had caught a venereal disease from one of his male lovers. She may have had some vague inkling before this of his feelings for other men. She had complained to her mother that he was 'cold'. But she probably had no real awareness until now of his lifelong homosexuality.

The revelation did not break the bond between them. Spring 1918 saw them spending their holiday together at Long Barn, sublimating their energies into planting sweet peas and dividing phlox. But perhaps it gave Vita licence to pursue other sexual interests – and constrained Harold to tolerate them.

Leonard (in the shadows) and Virginia Woolf, with the art critic Roger Fry between them. Fry – of whom Virginia later wrote a biography – was a key member of the Bloomsbury Group.

Many years later, in the 1960s, Vita would reproach Harold, as the elder, for not having explained their complicated sexuality more clearly to her. 'I was very young, and very innocent. I knew nothing about homosexuality. I didn't even know that such a thing existed – either between men or between women. You should have told me. You should have warned me.' But perhaps, outside Bloomsbury circles, such a conversation (at a time when male homosexuality was still illegal) was not possible so early in the twentieth century.

● ● ●

Through the last years of the war, as Virginia's diaries recorded planes going over Asheham, the ordinary work of Bloomsbury went on. Lytton Strachey brought out his *Eminent Victorians*, whose formal title belied his revolutionary approach to biography. Virginia's first novel *The Voyage Out*, published in 1915, had a reasonable reception but in spring 1917 Leonard, deciding it would be good for her to have a more practical occupation besides writing, purchased a printing press to set up on the dining room table, and an instruction book. The Hogarth Press was born.

The laborious ritualist business of typesetting was Virginia's job, owing to the tremor in Leonard's hands. So too was the binding in red thread, with beautiful paper covers: Virginia had done a bookbinding course as a hobby in her youth. It took them two and a half months to produce, a page at a time, fewer than 150 copies of their first publication, *Two Stories*, one by Virginia and one by Leonard. Their second work was Katherine Mansfield's *Prelude*, their third, a book of poems by a new young writer, one T.S. Eliot, with whom Virginia began a long professional relationship. They sold by subscription, and commissioned their artist friends to provide covers and illustrations. Though their original remit, Virginia said, had been to print up 'all our friends' stories', the Hogarth Press would go on to develop new writing of all sorts, including new political and economic theory. But meanwhile Virginia was turning her mind towards her next novel, *Night and Day*.

Virginia had a 'quicksand relationship' with the writer Katherine Mansfield (above), based on both camaraderie and rivalry.

When Armistice Day came, in November 1918, Harold Nicolson was told that he would be sent to the Peace Conference in Paris, but Vita – ever unpolitical – was preoccupied with personal affairs. Virginia and Leonard 'drifted' from Hogarth House to Trafalgar Square, finding the celebrations 'sordid and depressing'. In October 1919, Virginia brought out *Night and Day*, dedicated to her sister Vanessa. Contemplating the question of whether love and marriage were really essential for women, and set in the Edwardian world, it was seen by some as backward-looking.

Virginia's short story *Kew Gardens*, like many of her other works, represented a collaboration with Vanessa, who designed the cover.

The New Zealand-born writer Katherine Mansfield, a new friend and rival, was one who thought so. The 'quicksand' intimacy between these two women writers would comprise both admiration and jealousy, but Katherine was one of the few people with whom Virginia could discuss her work. A woman caring for writing, she said, was rare enough 'to give me the queerest sense of echo coming back to me from her mind'. Virginia was moving on as a writer – and change was coming in other directions, too.

The Hogarth Press was becoming more commercial. Demand for Virginia's groundbreaking, Impressionistic short story *Kew Gardens* had been such that they had had to turn to a commercial printer, instead of relying on their own small handpress. (They had had reluctantly to turn down James Joyce's *Ulysses* because it was too long for them to print alone, and no other printer would touch it, fearing prosecution for obscenity.) For more than a decade they would continue to use the two systems side by side, the handpress replaced in 1921 by a heavier machine in the basement of Hogarth House.

In 1919, with the lease on Asheham House coming to an end, Virginia and Leonard purchased Monk's House outside Lewes, just a few miles from Vanessa's home of Charleston. The Christmas after the war ended Vanessa had given birth to Angelica – Duncan's child – though the world was allowed to assume she was Clive's. But Duncan had now broken off his sexual affair with Vanessa, to her distress, though they continued to share a household at Charleston.

The Bloomsbury Group was no longer as tight-knit as it once had been. As Virginia told her diary: 'the worst of it is how seldom we meet … months pass without a sight … But when we do meet there is nothing to complain of.' In 1919, with his partners Vanessa and Duncan mostly in the country, Roger Fry decided to close the Omega Workshops. The very fact the term 'Bloomsbury' had come into wider currency was itself producing something of a backlash against what many saw as an inward-looking and elitist set. D.H. Lawrence complained that there was 'never, for one second … a crumb or grain of reverence' in them.

But when, in 1920, Desmond MacCarthy's wife Molly founded the Memoir Club, to promote the writing of autobiography, its original baker's dozen of members were the 'Old Bloomsbury' set, with the Woolfs, Vanessa and Duncan, Lytton Strachey, E.M. Forster and Maynard Keynes prominent among them. And the Memoir Club would provide the context for some of Virginia Woolf's most personal writing. It was to the Memoir Club that she described her abuse at the hands of her half-brother; the person presenting their memoir to the group was required to be completely candid, while one of the club rules declared that 'No one has the right to be shocked or aggrieved by what is said.'

By 1921 Virginia, publishing her short story collection *Monday or Tuesday*, was also working on what would become *Jacob's Room*, a novel imbued with her memories of her brother Thoby. She was seeking now to 'change the consciousness'. No realism any more, 'only thought and feelings, no cups and tables.' *Jacob's Room* was published on 26 October 1922, by the Hogarth Press, who would publish all her subsequent work.

One point of the Press had proved to be to give Virginia freedom, to liberate her from the fear of having an editor curb her more adventurous work. As 'the only woman in England free to write what I like' she no longer cared if reviews were mixed, if she

In 1919 Virginia and Leonard purchased Monk's House in the village of Rodmell as a country home. 'An unpretending house', Virginia called it.

was either 'a great writer or a nincompoop'. What she had always feared was being dismissed as negligible, and those days were past. She was writing 'something which I want to write; my own point of view'. Two months before she met Vita, she had found a voice of her own.

• • •

Vita had been through a time of crisis after her husband's revelations about his sexuality – a crisis the ever-present Violet Trefusis was quick to exploit. During one long night when they had talked for hours, Vita reports: 'Violet had struck the secret of my duality; she attacked me about it, and I made no attempt to conceal it from her or from myself … I talked out the whole of myself with absolute sincerity and pain.' Violet's response, as Vita describes it, was that of the expert seducer, but Vita herself was just drunk with liberation – 'the liberation of half my personality'. When she and Violet went away to Cornwall together, saying they wanted to see the spring flowers, Vita felt 'like a person translated, or re-born'.

Demanding, passionate, unfeeling towards those for whom she did not care, Violet would be the model for the abrasive Lady Montdore in Nancy Mitford's *Love in a Cold Climate*. She would also become the Russian princess Sasha in Virginia's *Orlando*, with her seduction, her wildness and her treachery. Harold said that Vita in Violet's hands became 'like a jellyfish addicted to cocaine'; that Violet herself was 'evil', 'like some fierce orchid – glimmering and stinking in the recesses of life – and throwing cadaverous sweetness on the morning breeze.'

By contrast, the word Vita would use for Harold was 'pure' (and, often, 'childlike'). After the apparent total harmony of their first years together, despite the impassioned intimacy they would share all their lives, there was now a discrepancy in what they both wanted, what they were able to provide. Harold wrote to Vita that he wished he were 'more violent and less affectionate'; Vita wrote of her wanderlust – in which she comprised a running away from the ordinary life, the humdrum, stagnation, 'bovine complacency'.

In the fantasy world where she and Violet now dwelt, they took on the Romany names of Mitya and Lushka. Vita (now often wearing the farm girl's uniform of breeches and gaiters) became also a young man called Julian. But then, Vita had always perceived two identities within herself – Violet called them Jekyll and Hyde. Vita said she was frightened of the Hyde side: 'it's so brutal and hard and savage, and Harold knows nothing of it; it would drive over his soul like an armoured chariot.' But this was the side to which Violet called. On 6 December, less than a month after Armistice, they set off for the South of France for three weeks. In fact, they stayed for four months – and very nearly did not come home at all.

Stopping off in Paris, they often went out as Julian and Lushka. Vita said she had never felt so free in her life. While Harold took the boys to Knole for Christmas, they went to Avignon and Monte Carlo. Violet ('that clammy little fiend', as Harold called her in one outspoken letter) made Vita promise to stay longer; it had been Violet's threat of suicide that drew Vita away at all. Under pressure from her parents and concerned by her abandonment of her children, Vita did return to England at the end of March. So too did Violet, who announced her engagement to Horse Guards Major Denys Trefusis – handsome, a war hero, with a spirit of adventure and very like Vita, Violet said. She told Vita that Denys had agreed that they should have 'merely brotherly relations'. But this would prove to be the calm before the storm.

In the spring of 1919, Vita was in London for the warm reception that greeted the publication of her first novel, *Heritage*. That same month her mother, unable any longer to endure the presence of Olive Rubens, left Knole forever, and Vita, fearful lest she would be unable to restrain herself from making a scene about Violet's marriage, went to join Harold in Paris. But Paris was where the Trefusises were to start their honeymoon, and Vita took to haunting the Ritz, where they were staying. As the new couple set out southwards – Violet writing of how her honeymoon made her 'a heartbroken nonentity, a lark with clipped wings'– Vita returned to Long Barn, finding refuge in the all-but-abandoned garden.

As Violet and Denys returned to England, however, they took a house only twenty miles from Long Barn. The affair continued. Harold too had a 'funny new friend' in Paris, a dressmaker, he wrote. In fact it was the couturier Edward Molyneux. But when in October Vita once again left for the continent with Violet, Harold was by no means prepared to accept that his life with Vita (as she had now declared, under pressure from Violet) was to be on a platonic footing: 'there can't be anything of that now – just now, I mean. Oh Hadji ("pilgrim" – her nickname for him), can't you realize a little?' In December the two women parted again, each to rejoin their husband.

In London, as 1920 dawned, Vita and Violet were still meeting every day, and it was Denys who forced the issue of whether they really wanted to live together forever. Violet asked for a week to think, but four days later phoned Vita, saying that it was now or never. Vita told Harold that – at the end of his fortnight's holiday, with the family at Knole – she would be leaving him for good. She did not understand his passivity. 'If I were you, and you were me, I would battle so hard to keep you …' As it was, she claimed she was forced 'to invent my own conviction out of your silence.' Harold would write later in life that Vita 'really does not care for the domestic affections. She would like life to be conducted on a series of *grandes passions*.' Or (as he added tellingly) 'she thinks she would.' In February the two women were to leave for France, never to return. But Vita sent Harold bulletins as to their progress all along the journey.

The voyage contained not only tragedy but farce. Violet set sail from Dover first – a gesture of propriety, as there had already been a great deal of talk – and Vita was to follow the next day. She found she was travelling in company with Denys, and a combination of seasickness and their shared love for Violet beat them into cordiality. On the train to Amiens, once they had rejoined Violet, Denys told Vita that Violet's mind was made up, and he would leave her forever. He took another train out of Amiens, leaving the two women alone. The next day, however, Violet's father Colonel Keppel arrived in Amiens, having wired for Denys.

Denys arrived in a two-seater plane, and Vita's mother had arranged that Harold should accompany him. The scene that followed was, Vita wrote, 'undignified and noisy to a degree'. But what made Vita 'half mad with pain' was when Harold told her that Violet and Denys had truly been husband and wife. The upshot was that Vita returned with Harold to Paris and, a fortnight later, to London.

Vita and Harold's marriage was now steady, though for Harold at least, the scars would never go away.

Even this was not the end – during the next six weeks Vita knew 'every variety of torment'. Late in March Vita once again went to join Violet in France and Italy. But Harold, catching up with them in Paris, persuaded them to return from this venture also, and it was perhaps the beginning of the end. That summer, after Violet had, as so often, successfully summoned back Vita's erring attention on the plea of her own distress and ill-health, Vita was telling her diary how much she longed for the peace of Long Barn. The following spring, January to March 1921, Vita and Violet were once again in the South of France together – this seemed like a connection that could never really be broken. But Vita had already, the previous summer, begun to write the autobiography which was surely some sort of goodbye.

While Violet, by arrangement between her husband and her mother, was sent to live abroad, Vita resumed life at Long Barn, slightly shaken by the whispers of scandal that now surrounded her name. She was writing again (she had been unable to do so, in the last days with Violet) and her new story, *The Heir*, reflected her feelings for Knole. Knole, with Harold, would be the enduring love of her life. She was also imagining into being her long poem *The Land* and beginning a history, *Knole and the Sackvilles*.

Vita and Harold's marriage was now steady, though for Harold at least, the scars would never go away. Though Vita sought always to reassure him with almost maternal tenderness, how could he not be alarmed in the months ahead? There were signs that the marriage of Vita's aristocratic friend and adorer Dorothy Wellesley was going badly (which might open a new phase of her friendship with Vita); 'Dottie' and Violet's close friend Pat Dansey seemed to be competing for Vita's attention; and Violet Trefusis herself was back in town. It must have been like living over a powder keg. But Vita's extra-marital relationships were now, in her son Nigel's opinion, 'no longer rockets, but slow-burning fuses with no explosives at the end. She loved more deeply, less passionately' than in the days when she had run away with Violet.

Harold could write about Vita's future affairs as her 'muddles'. (Virginia would describe her 'floundering habits'.) Vita called his, his 'fun'. 'Please don't fall too much in love with Mr Jebb,' she wrote to him once. 'I don't mind who you sleep with, so long as I may keep your heart!' Often his friend and hers would come to Long Barn on the same weekend, to the horror of Lady Sackville: 'Vita is absolutely devoted to Harold, but there is nothing whatever sexual between them, which is strange in such a young and good-looking couple. She is not in the least jealous of him, and willingly allows him to relieve himself with anyone.'

They had both thought through, to an almost mystical formula, their own definition of trust. Vita: 'we are sure of each other, in this odd, strange, detached, intimate, mystical relationship which we could never explain to any outside person.' Her 'creed' for him began with: 'To love me whatever I do.' It ended with: 'To give up everything and everybody for me in the last resort.' In the last resort, she would do as much for him.

Her affair with Violet was over, and other affairs would be less earth-shattering. But Vita still wanted something beyond the confines of Long Barn and her family, something that would not be a muddle. She was still afraid of the ordinary, the limited. Bloomsbury was not ordinary, Virginia Woolf's writing was not limited. Was Vita ready for a new adventure, but one which, this time, could live alongside her love for Harold?

Monk's House, Charleston
and Virginia Woolf's London

When, near the start of their friendship, Vita Sackville-West visited Monk's House, Virginia wrote that her aristocratic aura made it seem like a tumbledown barn. The Woolfs' country retreat was an inconvenient house, much smaller than Vanessa Bell's home at Charleston (a mere bicycling distance away) and, when they arrived, had been without electricity, bathroom, gas or an inside lavatory. It was, as Virginia wrote, 'an unpretending house, long & low, a house of many doors.'

Even Charleston — extraordinary visual feast though it was, decorated by the artists who lived and worked there — was, by Vita's standards, a place of 'high thinking and plain living'. But Charleston was nonetheless large enough to be a kind of Bloomsbury-in-the-country, where Maynard Keynes stayed so often he had his own designated bedroom before eventually taking a house just up the drive for himself and his new wife, the Russian ballerina Lydia Lopokova. Virginia would describe tea there taken 'from bright blue cups under the pink light of the giant hollyhock'.

Vanessa, Virginia wrote, presided over the most astonishing ménage at Charleston — 'Belgian hares, governesses, children, gardeners, hens, ducks and painting all the time, till every inch of the house is a different colour.' Monk's House, by contrast, allowed Virginia a tranquil life of mornings spent writing and afternoons reading and walking, with letters and her diary by the fire after tea. Virginia wrote in a shed-like room across the garden in the shadow of the Rodmell church, with views across the South Downs. She loved the landscape, the emptiness, bareness and colour, and the light, like 'the light beneath an alabaster

Charleston (opposite), where Vanessa Bell lived, came to represent the spiritual home of the Bloomsbury Group. One appeal of Monk's House (following pages) was the spacious garden, which would become Leonard's special project.

Above: Besides the lavish decoration undertaken at Charleston, the Bloomsbury artists also contributed many decorative items to Monk's House. Opposite: The view from Monk's House shows Virginia's outdoor writing room and the village church that broods over it.

bowl'. She would lie outside in the moonlight and the dawn. The Woolfs had spotted the notice of the house's sale almost by accident in the summer of 1919, just as they were forced to give up Asheham House. Virginia noted mockingly that she had told herself that the rooms were small, the kitchen bad and that 'monks are nothing out of the way'. This damped down her enthusiasm a little, but all objections were swept away by pleasure in 'the size & shape & fertility & wildness of the garden.'

After they bought the house at auction for £700 the garden would be predominantly Leonard's passion. It was he who would supervise the vegetable gardens, greenhouses, beehives and orchard. But Virginia would later write of how they both, in the house where they spent summers, holidays and 'divine fresh week ends', would both 'giggle and joke, and go and poke at roots, and plan beds of nasturtium'. For some years the house remained uncomfortable even by Bloomsbury standards. E.M. Forster, staying there, once set fire to his trousers trying to get warm

Tulips at Monk's House. Leonard's taste in flowers ran to the bold and colourful.

by the stove in his bedroom. But conveniences would be added one by one – as Virginia's books started to make money – even, in 1929, a two-storey extension. Virginia painted the walls herself – her relatives laughed at her choice of a virulent green paint – and Virginia would ask Vanessa to help furnish it in the style of the Omega Workshops, providing Vanessa with some financial support.

What Virginia most relished was the contrast between Monk's House and her London life. For Virginia adored London. She is most closely associated with the area that gave its name to the 'Bloomsbury' set, who indeed colonised the tall white houses around the squares to an extraordinary degree. Virginia wrote of how 46 Gordon Square 'is become a centre'. Her niece Angelica Bell wrote that having the Keyneses and Lytton Strachey's family, and Adrian Stephen with his wife and daughters, on their own side of Gordon Square – with 'the Woolves' just literally round the corner in Tavistock Square and other friends nearby – meant 'a family network that gave me the feeling that this part of London belonged to us.' (Lytton Strachey compared it, tellingly, to a Cambridge college.) Angelica remembered Gordon Square as a meeting ground, where a group of familiar figures could be seen watching the tennis players of an evening, and laughing at each other's jokes.

But it was not only Bloomsbury that Virginia loved, or pursued like a lover in her 'long romantic London walks'. She lamented its energy during the years Leonard's concern for her health confined them both to the limitations of Richmond. She loved to 'go adventuring among human beings' and had a particular affection for the City which best enshrines both London's dynamic future, and its past. 'Sometimes I should merely walk down Cheapside …' But that was enough. In Richmond, she memorably said, she felt 'like a leopard starved for blood'.

The Garden Room at Charleston. Duncan Grant painted the two kneeling figures above the fireplace. He and Vanessa Bell made every corner of the house a riot of pattern and imagery.

'London itself perpetually attracts, stimulates, gives me a play & a story & a poem, without any trouble, save that of moving my legs through the streets.' On the day she wrote that – 31 May, 1928 – she had just walked her cocker spaniel Pinker (a dog Vita had given her) to Gray's Inn Gardens via Red Lion Square and Great Ormond Street 'where a dead girl was found yesterday'. To walk alone in London, she said later, was 'the greatest rest'. Virginia would describe her habit as 'street haunting', and her enquiring spirit haunts many a street in London today.

PART II

1922–30
Orlando

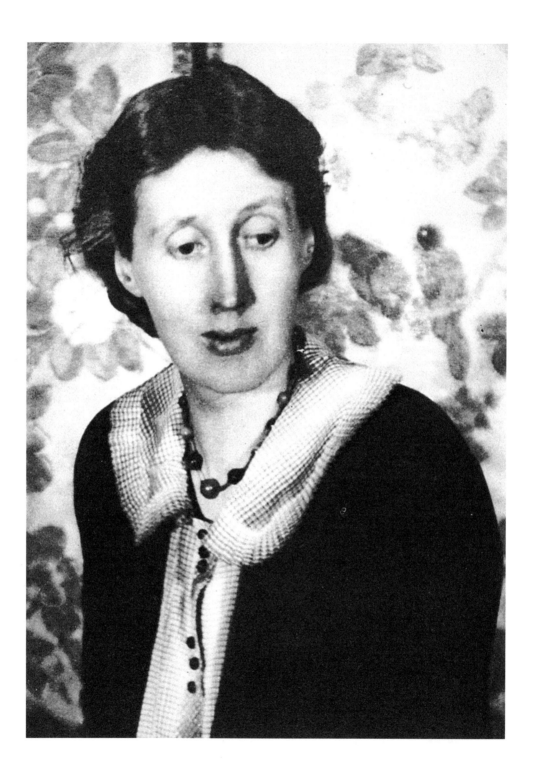

CHAPTER 4

∶ 1922–5 ∶

Virginia Woolf wrote in her diary on 3 Aug 1922: 'On the whole, L[eonard] & I are becoming celebrities … Mrs Nicolson thinks me the best woman writer – & I have almost got used to Mrs Nicolson's having heard of me.' It was December before Clive Bell introduced Virginia Woolf to his new acquaintance 'Mrs Nicolson' – an appellation Vita always detested – and Vita invited her to dine in Ebury Street four days later. But then the new friendship progressed with startling rapidity. Vita was ready to adore Virginia Woolf the writer. And Virginia – only beginning, at 40, to find her feet as a writer, only recently still convinced that Lytton or indeed Leonard had a better chance than she of being remembered – was ready to be adored.

Vita saw no reason to hide her new enthusiasm from Harold. She wrote to him that she simply adored Mrs Woolf, and so would he. That Virginia was so simple, she gave the impression 'of something big'. Virginia was completely without adornment or affectation, and dressed 'quite atrociously'. She seemed plain at first, but then 'a kind of spiritual beauty' made itself felt … 'Darling, I have quite lost my heart.'

Virginia told her diary the day after their meeting that she was 'muzzy headed', partly as a result of meeting the 'lovely gifted aristocratic Sackville West' – 'florid, moustached, parakeet coloured', as Virginia memorably described her, 'with all the supple ease of the aristocracy, but not the wit of the artist.' Vita wrote briskly, fifteen pages a day, Virginia noted with a mixture of admiration and reserve; knew everybody. 'But could I ever know her? I am to dine there on Tuesday.'

Vita, with 'no false shyness or modesty … asks for liqueur – has her hand on all the ropes – makes me feel virgin, shy, & schoolgirlish. Yet after dinner I rapped out opinions. She is a grenadier; hard, handsome, manly; inclined to double chin.'

This studio portrait from 1925 captures what everyone noted about Virginia – her thinness, her air of fragility and the magnetic eyes she turned away when listening to anyone. Vita noted also that she dressed 'quite atrociously'.

She was writing about Vita again on 2 January, after a New Year when Virginia had been in 'one of my moods, as the nurses used to call it'. She was feeling envious of her sister Vanessa's life and children – a recurring theme – and feeling, too, a little distance from Nessa, now spending much of her time abroad, and a little trapped that Leonard had reproached her for staying out late, for ignoring her health, for folly. She was afraid she and Leonard were becoming elderly. January 1923 saw the death from tuberculosis of Katherine Mansfield. Virginia feared they had something in common 'which I shall never find in anyone else. A sharpness, a sense of reality …'

Virginia and Leonard. She often smoked cheroots, or rolled her own cigarettes from strong shag tobacco.

The entrance of 'the new apparition Vita' was perhaps timely.

Virginia was looking for something new. She was in a mood to feel isolated at Monk's House, while in town the comparative seclusion of Richmond, on which Leonard insisted for Virginia's health, had made her feel 'tied, imprisoned, inhibited.' Months later, in her diary, she would still be countering Leonard's reservations about her urgent desire to move back into central London. For people of their age – 'which is full summer' – to dread risk seemed 'pusillanimous'; the next ten years must see them press on into either fame or bankruptcy. Vita would encourage her to be a little more adventurous on even the most practical levels – to dress more smartly and spend money. Later in her friendship with Vita, Virginia would acknowledge how Vita opened new horizons for her. 'I use my friends rather as giglamps: there's another field I see; by your light.'

One of the few photographs of Virginia (left) and Vita together, taken by Leonard Woolf. A love of dogs would be a bond between the pair.

After Virginia had been ill, in and out of bed for a week, in mid-February came a surprise visit from 'the Nicolsons. She is a pronounced Sapphist, & may … have an eye on me, old though I am.' Vita's diary notes: 'Dined with Virginia at Richmond … she says that love makes everyone a bore, but the excitement of life lies in "the little moves" nearer to people.' But perhaps, Vita added, 'she feels this because she's an experimentalist in humanity and has no *grande passion* in her life …'

In mid-March the Nicolsons dined at 46 Gordon Square, meeting the Bloomsbury set, and Virginia felt that that bright light did not show them to their advantage: 'we judged them both incurably stupid.' Harold was bluff but obvious, Vita stiff. Vita, with her strong establishment connections, had written a miniature volume, *A Note of Explanation*, for the bookshelves of Queen Mary's famous dolls' house, now at Windsor. It was a whimsical tale, whose fairytale heroine witnessed Aladdin's palace being built and attended Cinderella's ball, before moving into the dolls' house with all its twentieth-century conveniences. Vita suggested Virginia should contribute a story, too – but instead, the idea of an undying spirit inhabiting a house would perhaps make its way into Virginia's *Orlando*.

> *The affair would wreck his marriage – but in the end Vita was not prepared to allow it to wreck hers.*

By the autumn of 1923, however, Vita had a different romance on her mind. She had known Geoffrey Scott since childhood but when she went stay with him and his wife Lady Sybil in their villa above Florence she responded ardently to his sudden declaration of love. But her passion burnt itself out faster than his. The following spring he was offering to renounce everything for her. The affair would wreck his marriage – but in the end Vita was not prepared to allow it to wreck hers. He was, as Nigel Nicolson puts it, to be 'replaced by someone to whom he could not hold a candle, a woman, a genius', and one whose romance with Vita could work in tandem with Vita's love for Harold.

Virginia would look back, five years later, remembering how Geoffrey sat in a mews off Regent's Park, fuming, while Vita 'sat in Tavistock Square talking to me.' In March 1924 the Woolfs moved to 52 Tavistock Square, taking the top two floors for themselves and the basement for the Press and Virginia's study, with a solicitor's office occupying the space in between. Seven years after the Hogarth Press had started, the 'amateurish, ramshackle concern' continued to grow. Thirty-four books were announced in their 1925 list. Now the bestselling Vita was to join their stable of authors.

Vanessa Bell painted this watercolour of Virginia in 52 Tavistock Square, and gave it to Leonard as a Christmas present. The Woolfs moved to Tavistock Square from Richmond in 1924.

Virginia rejoiced in the return to Bloomsbury. 'London thou art a jewel of jewels, & jasper of jocunditie – music, talk, friendship, city views, books, publishing, something central & inexplicable, all this is now within my reach.' That summer she also visited Knole with Vita, not put off even by the fact that Geoffrey Scott and Dottie Wellesley were in the party too.

'All these ancestors & centuries, & silver & gold, have bred a perfect body', Virginia wrote of Vita afterwards. 'She is stag like, or race horse like, save for the face, which pouts, & has no very sharp brain, But as a body hers is perfection … it's the breeding of Vita's that I took away with me as an impression'. Virginia had always been as drawn to the Elizabethans as Vita herself. (The first volume of Virginia's book of essays on literature, *The Common Reader*, which would be published the following year, featured a chapter on 'The Elizabethan Lumber Room'.)

Vita – in the Dolomites later that month, and writing *Seducers in Ecuador* for the Hogarth Press – noted shrewdly how Virginia used people as copy: 'you like people through the brain better than through the heart.' Virginia wrote back that she enjoyed the intimate letter, which had given her a good deal of pain – 'which I've no doubt is the first stage of intimacy.'

Even Leonard described Vita at this point as being literally in the prime of life, 'an animal at the height of its powers, a beautiful flower in full bloom. She was very handsome, dashing, aristocratic, lordly, almost arrogant.' To him it was this element was that made intimacy difficult. The Woolfs used to tell Vita she was only really comfortable in a castle, while that was the only place, Leonard said, in which he could never feel at home.

But Virginia relished the very incongruity of Vita's visit to Monk's House, gliding through the village in a large new blue Austin car, with 'a dressing case all full of silver & night gowns wrapped in tissue'. She liked Vita's being 'a perfect lady, with all the dash & courage of the aristocracy, & less of its childishness than I expected.' She even admired *Seducers in Ecuador*, in which Vita had 'shed the old verbiage', and found 'some sort of glimmer of art'. Temperate praise, perhaps – yet was Vita not also a 'mother, wife, great lady, hostess, as well as scribbling', Virginia asked? 'How little I do of all that …' Virginia's appreciation of Vita's writing, in general, would remain chiefly that of a publisher for a bestselling author. But she admired Vita's 'manly good sense & simplicity … Oh yes, I like her; could tack her on to my equipage for all time; & suppose if life allowed, this might be a friendship of a sort.'

> *'I rather marvel at her skill, & sensibility; for is she not mother, wife, great lady, hostess, as well as scribbling?'*

That winter Virginia confessed to Jacques Raverat that she was more and more committed to friendship but that '*sexual* relations bore me more than they used'. Love, she wrote, was a disease; a frenzy; an epidemic; oh but how dull, how monotonous, and reducing its young men and women to what abysses of mediocrity!'

Virginia described Vita as 'a grenadier; hard, handsome, manly.'

Virginia was about to bring out *Mrs Dalloway*, an account of one June day in 1923, and of the party being prepared by society hostess Clarissa Dalloway. The experiences of the traumatised war veteran Septimus Warren Smith in the novel echoes Virginia's own. Urged by a Harley Street specialist to think about himself as little as possible, condemned to endless rest and separation from his wife, and dismissed as a coward by his GP, he jumps to his death. But there are echoes of Virginia too in Clarissa Dalloway's girlhood experience with her old friend Sally Seton. Clarissa recalled the girlhood kiss they shared as 'the most exquisite moment of her whole life'. 'If one could be friendly with women', Virginia wrote, 'what a pleasure – the relationship so secret & private compared with relations with men.'

She already had the concept for her next novel, *To the Lighthouse*, which she raced through over the next year, though sometimes thwarted into silence and sickness by the personal aspect of the material. It would have her father's character 'done complete' in it, her mother's, St Ives, childhood – '& all the usual things I put in – life, death, &c.' – Virginia told her diary before writing it. 'But the centre is father's character, sitting in a boat, reciting We perished, each alone, while he crushes a dying mackerel'. The two sections of the book – the first, golden, long summer holiday and the brief later return to the holiday home – were linked by a long and consciously experimental passage, 'Time Passes', during which, in a mere parenthesis, Mrs Ramsay dies. Virginia 'had the idea that I will invent a new name for my books to supplant "novel". A new – by Virginia Woolf. But what? Elegy?'

In *To the Lighthouse*, The Ramsays' holiday on the Isle of Skye evoked the Stephens' holidays in St Ives; Mrs Ramsay is Julia Stephen but also Vanessa, Virginia said. But perhaps the almost erotic devotion other characters feel for Mrs Ramsay was charged by Virginia's feeling for Vita, whom she compared to a lighthouse: 'fitful, sullen, remote'. Writing Mrs Ramsay, Virginia would later say, had ended the obsession with her mother. Did Vita play any part in that?

When in the autumn Virginia was unwell, Vita wrote to urge the advantages of Long Barn 'as a convalescent home'. At the end of November came the news that Vita was 'doomed' to go to Persia, Harold's next diplomatic posting, and Virginia minded the thought so much 'that I conclude I am genuinely fond of her'. The best thing about these illnesses, she noted, was that they 'loosened the soil around the roots' – allowed for the possibility of change. Change – growth – in this relationship was coming on apace.

On 7 December Virginia was abashed to find herself almost tearful: 'partly that devil Vita. No letter. No visit. No invitation to Long Barn ... if I do not see her now, I shall not – ever: for the moment for intimacy will be gone, next summer.' Vita, in the midst of her preparations to leave for Persia, was writing to Harold in a different key. She had brought Virginia to Long Barn, and she was 'an exquisite companion', but:

'Please don't think that
(a) I shall fall in love with Virginia
(b) Virginia will fall in love with me
(c) Leonard " " " "   " "
(d) I shall fall   " " " Leonard

Because it is not so.'

This portrait of Vita reflects the swashbuckling, aristocratic quality that drew Virginia to her. 'She is stag like, or race horse like', Virginia said.

Virginia was, Vita wrote two days later, 'one of the most mentally exciting people I know'. Their friendship had come on by leaps and bounds in those two days, but though Vita loved her she could not be 'in love' with her … And yet it was during the two days Virginia spent alone at Long Barn with Vita, before Leonard joined them, that – according to Vita's later report to Harold – their relationship became physical. Although Vita has usually been taken for the more active partner, the two women would later joke about 'the explosion which happened on the sofa' when Virginia 'behaved so disgracefully'.

The long and enraptured description of Vita that Virginia wrote in her diary explored the nature of her glamour. In the unlikely setting of the grocer's shop in Sevenoaks, Vita shone 'with a candle lit radiance'. She stalked 'on legs like beech trees' – Virginia would continue to be much taken with Vita's legs – 'pink glowing, grape clustered, pearl hung.'

But Vita's appeal for Virginia was not wholly physical. Virginia was drawn to Vita's 'maturity and full breastedness' – the sense that Vita was 'in full sail on high tides', while Virginia herself was confined (by her own constraints, and by Leonard's watchful care) to a quiet life in the backwaters.

Virginia saw a link between Vita's ability to visit Chatsworth, represent her country, control chow dogs, and her very motherhood – 'her being in short (what I have never been) a real woman.' It is reminiscent of the tone in which she had written about that other 'real woman', Vanessa, just after Nessa's marriage, years before.

The much-labelled suitcase from Vita's collection at Sissinghurst evokes the glamour of her travels in Persia.

Vita herself was aware of this, Virginia noted, '& so lavishes on me the maternal protection which, for some reason, is what I have always most wished from everyone.' What she got from Leonard, and from Vanessa, she drew also from Vita, albeit 'in a more clumsy external way.'

In this long entry in Virginia's diary, it is interesting to see Leonard's tolerance of the affair. Ever nervous of anything that might agitate Virginia, he had nonetheless this time been the

Vita on a mule. Her trip across the Bakhtiari mountains would become her travel book *Twelve Days*. She wrote to Virginia of how she had slept in ruined huts, and lost all sense of civilisation.

one to tell her that her 'fears and refrainings … my usual self-consciousness in intercourse with people who mayn't want me & so on' were all 'sheer fudge'.

By the same token Harold – with bitter experience behind him, and with a very different wife to deal with – wrote to Vita on 8 January 1926, 'I am not really bothered about Virginia and think you are probably very good for each other. I only feel that you have not got *la main heureuse* [a light touch] in dealing with married couples.' He was thinking of Geoffrey Scott, who had rung Vita, hysterically, to say goodbye.

As Vita set off for Persia, she was writing to Virginia even from the Dover train. From Milan she wrote that she was 'reduced to a thing that wants Virginia' – it was incredible how essential to her Virginia had become. In the power balance of their relationship, that revelation might not help her cause – 'But oh my dear, I can't be clever and standoffish with you: I love you too much for that.' In the event she would relish – and describe in her book *Passenger to*

Teheran – both the exoticism of the adventure and wonderful wildness of Persia itself.

Virginia, left behind, had noted in her diary how 'I feel a lack of stimulus, of marked days, now Vita is gone'. She would later tell Vita that she had been startled and terrified by her own unhappiness. But perhaps it was the very geographical distance which had been looming between them that had allowed Virginia, uncharacteristically, to go as far in this relationship as she had done. A few months later, at the end of May, as the time neared for Vita's return, Virginia was querying the very nature of her relations with Vita, left so ardent in January – '& now what?' Virginia asked herself whether she was indeed in love with Vita – 'But what is love?' Vita's being 'in love' with Virginia was itself an appeal – it 'excites & flatters, & interests.'

Five days later, after Vita's return, Virginia was recording 'the shock of meeting after absence: how shy one is; how disillusioned by the actual body'. Vita seemed more mature but shabbier, quieter and shyer; she, Virginia was chattering, 'to prevent her thinking "Well, is this all?" as she was bound to think, having declared herself so openly in writing.' The element of detachment would remain, on both sides, maybe.

On 12 June 1926 Vita wrote to Harold that she was going to Rodmell for two nights since Harold was away and Virginia did not want to be alone. The Woolfs had put in a bathroom on the proceeds of *Mrs Dalloway* and Vita described how they would run upstairs and pull the lavatory chain, for the sheer pleasure of hearing the flush. She and Virginia picnicked off coffee, boiled eggs, wine and cherries. Virginia – sitting opposite, embroidering a design of Vanessa Bell's – looked up from time to time to say, 'now let us talk about copulation.'

Virginia wrote to Nessa, perhaps rather boastfully, that 'the June nights are long and warm; the roses flowering; and the garden full of lust and bees, mingling in the asparagus beds.' Vita was having once again to assure Harold that she was in no 'muddles' (love affairs). 'Virginia – not a muddle exactly; she is a busy and sensible woman. But she does love me, and I did sleep with her at Rodmell. That does not constitute a muddle though.' Harold replied: 'Oh my dear, I do hope that Virginia is not going to be a muddle. It is like smoking over a petrol tank.' Vita strove to reassure Harold, telling him that Violet Trefusis had been 'a madness of which I should never again be capable'.

For Harold to worry about her relationship with Virginia was 'simply laughable', she reassured him. Love for Virginia was a very different thing to love for Violet – 'a mental thing, a spiritual thing if you like, an intellectual thing, and she inspires a feeling of tenderness which I suppose is because of her funny mixture of hardness and softness – the hardness of her mind, and her terror of going mad again.' Vita felt protective – besides being flattered, as she frankly said, by Virginia's love. She was, moreover, 'scared to death of arousing physical feelings in her, because of the madness. I don't know what effect it would have, you see: and that is a fire with which I have no wish to play.'

Virginia, Vita wrote, had never 'lived with' anyone but Leonard, and that was 'a terrible failure and abandoned quite soon.' So she, Vita, was sagacious, 'though probably I would be less sagacious if I were more tempted, which as at least frank! … I have gone to bed with her (twice), but that's all; and I told you that before, I think.'

This is the picture – of a strong, sensual Vita restraining herself because of Virginia's otherworldly fragility – that has been preserved for posterity – but it is arguable that the letters of the

> *Virginia would later tell Vita that she had been startled and terrified by her own unhappiness.*

two women tell a more complex story. Certainly sex would continue to be at least a joke between them. After an unsuccessful visit the Woolfs made to the Nicolsons in Berlin – later, in 1929, after Harold was posted there as First Secretary – Vita declared that the reason Virginia had become ill afterwards was not just the 'flu but 'SUPPRESSED RANDINESS'. Mere badinage? The subordination of feelings? Maybe.

Of course Virginia was always fragile after finishing a novel, and *To the Lighthouse* was no exception. Waking at three one morning, she described for her diary a painful wave all but sweeping her away. A consciousness of the children Vanessa had and she did not; of her failure (as she saw it) as a writer; even of how her friends had laughed at her taste in green paint. 'Now take a pull of yourself', she adjured herself, stepping back from the brink.

That same month Vita brought out *The Land*, in many ways an unashamedly old-fashioned poem, hymning 'the cycle of my country's year', the Kentish agricultural round, the techniques and trades from a world before mechanisation. Their worlds were still different. Virginia was introducing Vita more into Bloomsbury, which she called Gloomsbury, and joking about how she couldn't come to Knole 'without a pin to my hair or a stocking to my foot'. Vita for her part wrote to Harold that Virginia's conversation made her feel 'as though my mind were being held against a grindstone.' Vita was, she confessed, 'rather proud of having caught such a big silver fish'. Virginia appears in letter after letter to the absent Harold, and Vita asks whether this annoys him? It's just that 'her friendship does enrich me so … I don't think I have ever loved anybody so much, in the way of friendship'.

Harold was still concerned lest this should be a 'muddle'. 'It is such a powder magazine. I am far more worried for Virginia and Leonard's sake than for ours.' He feared lest Virginia should be made ill, he feared a little that Virginia's company might make his seem dull. 'But my dominant idea is one of pleasure that the rich ores of your nature should be brought to light – I *know* that it does you moral and mental good to be with her and be loved by her and that is all that matters.' He even wrote to Virginia, with notable generosity, that he was glad Vita had come under an influence 'so stimulating and so sane'. He longed only for Vita's life to be as rich and as sincere as possible, so Virginia need have no worries. 'I loathe jealousy as I loathe all forms of disease.'

Virginia had come to much the same conclusion. Her diary recorded Vita sitting on the floor, in her velvet jacket and silk shirt, while Virginia played with her pearls, knotting the ropes into a heap of 'great lustrous eggs'. There might be room for a good many relationships in a life, and hers with Vita was a spirited, creditable affair, she congratulated herself, 'innocent (spiritually) & all gain, I think: rather a bore for Leonard, but not enough to worry him.'

But as so often, the placid picture painted, even to Virginia's diary, was not the whole story: Vita was now sending one letter to Virginia inside another, cooler one, to shield the more intimate communication from Leonard's eyes. And it was clearly the supposedly stronger Vita who had been reproaching Virginia with distance: 'dont you see, donkey West, that you'll be tired of me one of these days (I'm so much older) and so I have to take my little precautions', Virginia replied. 'But donkey West knows she has broken down more ramparts than anyone.' And was there not, she asked, something 'reserved, muted' in Vita too – something that affected both her human relationships and her writing? Clearly there were insecurities on both sides.

As Vita set off to Persia again in the new year, she sent Virginia a stream of frantic letters. From Ebury Street before she left: 'I feel torn in a thousand pieces – it is bloody – I can't tell you how I hate leaving you.' The postscript begged

Virginia to call her honey in her letters, to go on loving her … A telegram from Vita, a letter on the train to Dover ('I wish I didn't love you so much. No I don't though; that's not true.') From somewhere near Hanover, as the train bore her on, she wrote a letter including a tiny sketch of a crossroads, saying she had been at a crossroads when she met Virginia – bad novels or good poetry. 'You do like me to write well. Don't you? And I do hate writing badly'. From Moscow, that she bore Virginia a grudge for having spoiled her for everybody else's company.

Virginia wrote back more restrainedly that it was 'nice' to get so many letters and telegrams, that Vita has demoralised her. She spoke of herself as a 'eunuch' – an onlooker who sees more of the game. 'Here in my cave I see lots of things you blazing beauties make invisible by the light of your own glory.' But in February she admitted that she had settled down to wanting Vita 'doggedly, dismally, faithfully – I hope that pleases you.' In March she was asking herself: 'Now what would happen if I let myself go over. Answer me that. Over what? You'll say. A precipice marked V.'

From Teheran Vita sent letters complaining how little she was suited to a diplomatic life. Dinner parties with too much to eat and drink, calls, the long wait for the post, making desultory conversation with subalterns. But before leaving she did, on foot and muleback, make the trip across the Bakhtiari mountains to the Persian Gulf that would become her travel book *Twelve Days*. She wrote to Virginia of how she had 'slept in ruined huts; made fires of pomegranate wood and dried camel-dung; boiled eggs; lost all sense of civilisation'. She wrote too of waking in the Persian dawn to say to herself, 'Virginia …' and of their plan to go abroad together in October: 'sun and cafes all day, and ? all night.'

Virginia was awaiting the May publication of *To the Lighthouse*. When it came out: 'So far Vita praises, Dotty enthuses; an unknown Donkey writes.' The praise she most valued was from Vanessa, 'She says it is an amazing portrait of mother … found the rising of the dead almost painful'. A month out, and she was able to record that the book was 'much more nearly a success, in the usual sense of the word, than any other book of mine.' Soon, free again, 'my deep dive into my own mind will begin.' On 29 June both the Woolfs and the Nicolsons were in a party that travelled north to Yorkshire to witness the total eclipse of the sun. Extraordinary, Virginia wrote. 'We had seen the world dead.' But maybe *To the Lighthouse* represented a rebirth of a sort – and maybe Vita was a part of that.

That July of 1927, with Harold back from Teheran, both Woolfs went to stay with the Nicolsons at Long Barn. 'Such opulence & freedom', Virginia told her diary, recalling the silver and the servants, the fires and furniture, the books and

Virginia saw Vita as 'pink glowing, grape clustered, pearl hung. That is the secret of her glamour, I suppose … her being so much in full sail on the high tides'.

the biscuits – the general impressions of stepping out onto 'a rolling gay sea'. For the weekend at least, she said, it seemed as if 'the anxious worn life had suddenly been set on springs' as it went bounding gaily away.

Yet for all that she preferred her own room, with 'more effort & life in it'. She saw the Nicolsons' future as ripe and golden in a night of 'indigo blue, with a soft golden moon. They lack only what we have – some cutting edge; some invaluable idiosyncrasy, intensity, for which I would not have all the sons & all the moons in the world.'

A few years before, Virginia had written to Vita: 'In all London, you and I alone like being married.' As she told her diary once: 'I snuggled in to the core of my life, which is this complete comfort with L., & there found everything so satisfactory & calm that I revived myself, & got a fresh start; feeling entirely immune.' 'L. may be severe; but he stimulates', she wrote on another occasion. 'Anything is possible with him.'

Many years later – and just one of their many avowals to each other – Vita would write to Harold of how they had from the conventional point of view been as unfaithful to each other as could be, yet no two people could love each more after all. The two women could even appreciate each other's husbands, up to a point. Vita would write that Leonard was tiresome but 'irresistibly young and attractive', Virginia that Harold was 'not Vita's match; but honest and cordial …

flimsy compared with Leonard'. (He had, she memorably said on another occasion, a mind that bounces when he drops it.) They would be less tolerant of each other's relations with other women.

When it came to other affairs, Vita was no more constrained by her love for Virginia than by her marriage to Harold. Even as Virginia watched her accept the Hawthornden Prize for *The Land*, Vita was falling in love with Mary Campbell, wife to the poet Roy, to whom the Nicolsons had lent the gardeners' cottage attached to Long Barn. (He later wrote a bitter poem, *The Georgiad*, about 'intellectuals without intellect/And sexless folk whose sexes intersect'.)

The rules of the game they made for themselves suggested that this was one that two could play. When Vita admitted that she liked making Virginia jealous, Virginia warned her to 'be a careful dolphin in your gambolling, or you'll find Virginia's soft crevices lined with hooks.' They both described how they would make the other jealous with letters from other admirers. When Vita declared 'I won't be trifled with. I really mean this', Virginia was equally uncompromising: 'I wont belong to the two of you … if Dotty [Dorothy Wellesley]'s yours, I'm not.' In reality the sexual freedom was inevitably all on Vita's side. But Virginia had a new weapon in her hands – one which might give her a measure of control over Vita, even as it celebrated and soothed her.

CHAPTER 5

⋮ 1926–30 ⋮

On 9 October 1927 Virginia wrote to Vita. The day before she had been in despair, unable to screw out a word, until she dipped her pen in the ink and wrote, as if automatically: '*Orlando: A Biography*'.

'But listen; suppose Orlando turns out to be Vita; and it's all about you and the lusts of your flesh and the lure of your mind … Shall you mind? Say yes, or No.' There could be only one answer: Vita was, she said, thrilled and terrified, but what fun! Vita's son Nigel Nicolson would call Virginia's *Orlando* 'the longest and most charming love letter in literature.'

The book follows the fortunes of a young nobleman, born in the Elizabethan age into the inheritance of a great house. Miraculously, *Orlando* would survive through more than three centuries, so that the story ends only on the very day on the book's publication: 11 October 1928. Orlando at that time is still only 36 – Vita's age – and loving the same things as she does: writing poetry; trees; salukis, spaniels and elkhounds; the heraldic leopards of the Sackville family crest, pearls and red Spanish wine.

But the real twist of *Orlando* would be that, in the course of a long sleep, the nobleman is changed into a woman, without losing her identity – or her inheritance. In fiction (and Vita, all her life, explored her own identity in her fictional writings) Virginia would give back to Vita what the law denied her: possession of her beloved Knole.

Virginia had in fact told her diary a few days before she wrote to Vita that she was contemplating 'a biography beginning in the year 1500 and continuing to the present day, called *Orlando*: Vita, only with a change about from one sex to another.' As she began to write, Virginia needed to study Vita in a new way. 'About your teeth now and your temper. Is it true you grind your teeth at night? Is it true you love giving pain?' Orlando had 'cheeks covered in peach down' – Virginia

Sally Potter's 1992 film of *Orlando* cast Tilda Swinton as the eponymous hero. Virginia based the character directly on Vita, whom she envisaged striding through her ancestral woods with a pack of elkhounds at her heels.

Vita's adored Knole would be the model for the 'great house of his fathers' which Orlando loved.

had compared the down on Vita's face to a velvety plant. Orlando had wonderfully shapely legs – Virginia harped on Vita's bold stride and the splendour of her legs, 'running like slender pillars up into her trunk'.

Orlando was in love with his great house just as Vita was with Knole. 'Courts and buildings, grey, red, plum colour'; chapel and belfry, cedars and lawns, the whole ordered, 'noble and humane', as Virginia would describe it in the book.

Perhaps even – as Orlando is sent by Charles II as ambassador to Constantinople – his wanderings with the gypsies, his snuffing of the 'acrid, sharp smell of the streets' recalls Vita's adventures in Persia, when the boredom of the role of diplomat's wife was assuaged by the glamour of the east. Several of Vita's previous lovers would be in the book – Violet Trefusis as wild Russian beauty Sasha, and Lord Lascelles as the hee-hawing Archduchess (or Archduke) Harriet. Harold too was there, flatteringly portrayed as the explorer Marmaduke Bonthrop Shelmerdine: a man as 'strange and subtle' as a woman, just as Orlando was a woman 'as tolerant and free-spoken' as a man.

Before the end of October Virginia was, she told her diary, 'in the thick of the greatest rapture known to me' – making up phrases, contriving scenes. By the end of the year she had realised the writing process was not going to be as speedy as she had thought, but still held to her first idea of its tone: 'half laughing, half serious: with great splashes of exaggeration.' She went with Vita to Knole to research the book.

But Knole itself was suffering a change: one Vita had always dreaded, one that brought home to her the disadvantages of her female sex. In January 1928 her father was dying, and the law that governed titles and entailed estates meant that, as a woman, Vita could not succeed him. The knowledge had cast a blight over her childhood – more than two decades later she would still be lamenting to Harold that she had not been born her father's son. As Lionel, third Baron Sackville, died slowly and in agony, Vita nursed him, in company with Lionel's longtime mistress Olive Rubens, but that only divided her further from her mother Victoria, Lionel's estranged wife. From now on Vita – whose name meant 'Life' – had to live with the knowledge that her mother had renamed her 'Vipa'.

Virginia was a constantly supportive presence. Vita told Clive Bell that she had discovered Virginia had a heart of pure gold. 'I shall never forget her sweetness to me through all this time.' On 28 January Lionel died, leaving Vita undisputed rule of the house for just a few days before it passed to an uncle to whom she was not close. She would later tell her son Ben that those few days 'marked a turning point in my life.' But Virginia recorded sympathetically that when Vita left Knole, behind the old carthorses that dragged Lionel's body to the family burial place at Withyham, she said that she went forever. Only *Orlando* could restore to her Knole's future – and its past.

> *More than two decades later Vita would still be lamenting to Harold that she had not been born her father's son.*

But perhaps *Orlando* was for Virginia a way not only of celebrating Vita, but also of controlling her. Of rewriting on her own terms a liaison which – given their very different temperaments – Vita was always likely to take more cavalierly than she.

That possibility is reflected in the violence of the language in which they discussed the book. On 20 March Virginia wrote to Vita: 'Did you feel a sort of tug, as if your neck was being broken on Saturday last at 5 minutes to one? That was when he [Orlando] died'. She voiced what must have been Vita's fears when she asked how her own feelings towards Vita would now be changed. I've lived in you all these months – coming out, what are you really like? Do you exist? Have I made

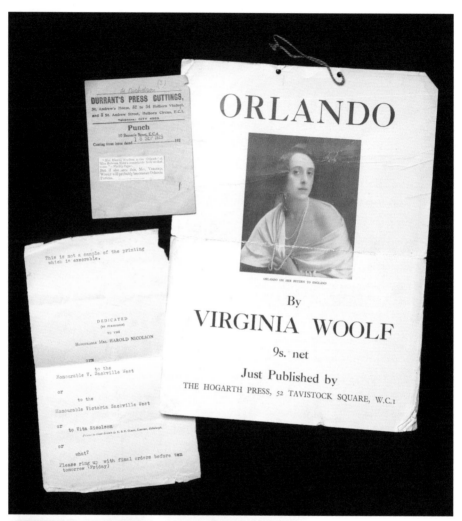

ORLANDO

ORLANDO ON HER RETURN TO ENGLAND

By
VIRGINIA WOOLF

9s. net

Just Published by
THE HOGARTH PRESS, 52 TAVISTOCK SQUARE, W.C.1

Vita kept a box of cuttings about Virginia's work, and memorabilia of *Orlando* in particular. She was photographed (below, left and right) to provide the illustrations of Orlando's later career.

Virginia visiting Vita and her sons at Knole while writing *Orlando*. She was struck anew by the way the house made the past seem alive.

you up?' Vita, 'terrified', wrote back that she had always foreseen this danger. '*I won't be fictitious. I won't be loved solely in an astral body, or in Virginia's world.*'

Some things no fiction could invent. Vita's mother was becoming increasingly paranoid, convinced she would not get her dues from the estate of her estranged husband Lionel. In April, while Vita was in conference with the family lawyers, her mother unexpectedly appeared, screaming that she wanted back all the jewels she had ever given Vita.

Virginia recorded indignantly how Vita, standing in the street by her mother's car, had been made to take the pearl necklace from her throat, cut it in two and hand over the twelve central pearls to her mother. 'Thief, liar, I hope you'll be killed by an omnibus – so "my honoured Lady Sackville" addressed her, trembling with rage in the presence of a secretary & a solicitor & a Chauffeur. The woman is said to be mad.'

Vita reacted by tossing her head, taking Virginia to the zoo and saying she would make her own money. But the wound took a long time to heal. Perhaps it would be soothed when Vita read of Orlando travelling with the gypsies and breaking off pearls from her string to pay her way.

That summer, as she several times visited Vita and Harold at Long Barn, Virginia commissioned the last of the pictures with which the first edition of *Orlando* would be illustrated. (Vita and Virginia also went together to have their ears pierced.) The image of Orlando as a young boy was taken from a portrait hanging on the walls of Knole: that of Sasha was Virginia's niece, Angelica Bell, in exotic dress. But the Orlando who – now transformed into a woman – returned from Constantinople to England, was Vita herself cast as a Lely portrait. Uncharacteristically – and, she said, uncomfortably – she was photographed in a loose wrap under her signature pearls. She was photographed again, in different costume, for the Orlando of the Victorian age, but 'Orlando at the Present Time' was Vita as she might be seen every day, leaning against a country gate and holding the leash of her beloved dogs.

Vita was not allowed to see the book in progress, a fact less strange to her for the fact that she herself often kept her current work secret even from her family. Both women were aware, as they agreed to go on holiday to France together that autumn, that the dynamics of their relationship were in flux, and that *Orlando* might speed the process. In August Vita wrote to Virginia that if 11 October – publication day – 'is to see the end of our romance, it would be as well to make the most of the short time that remains to us.' Virginia told her diary she was 'alarmed of 7 days alone with Vita: interested; excited, but afraid – she may find me out, I her out.' Later, she noted that they didn't … Were they now already on emotionally safer ground, or would *Orlando* mean fresh adventures together in the years ahead?

Virginia sent Vita a specially bound presentation copy of the book, as well as giving her the manuscript. On 11 October Vita wrote to Harold in a storm of pleasure and confusion, halfway through reading the book. 'I scarcely slept with excitement all night, and woke up feeling as though it were my birthday, or wedding day, or something unique.' She felt somehow, she told him, 'that Knole knows about *Orlando*, and is pleased.'

On the same day she wrote to Virginia: 'I am completely dazzled, bewitched, enchanted, under a spell. It seems to me the loveliest, wisest, richest book that I have ever read …' Harold spoke as enthusiastically.

That summer, after a 'good rather happy' visit to Long Barn, Virginia had written in her diary: 'I'm interested by the gnawing down of strata in friendship; how one passes unconsciously to different terms; takes things easier; don't mind at all hardly about dress or anything; scarcely feel it an exciting atmosphere, which, too, has its drawback from the "fizzing" point of view: yet is saner, perhaps deeper.'

The two women themselves were surely aware of the complex messages behind the book. Through *Orlando*, Virginia had reclaimed Knole for Vita – but had

Vita's son Nigel Nicolson called *Orlando* 'the longest and most charming love letter in literature.'

she also reasserted her own possession of Vita herself? Their relationship would continue to be a work in progress – Vita had written once about how women were more prepared to work at shaping friendships than are men. There was change here but there was also hope. As Vita also tells Virginia: 'all sorts of different landscapes seem to open, whichever way I look.'

●●●

Different landscapes were opening for Virginia, too. Weeks after *Orlando* was published she went twice to Cambridge – once with Leonard, once with Vita – to lecture on women and fiction. After the talk at Girton College, where Vita had heard her speaking to Girton's 'starved but valiant' young women 'destined to become schoolmistresses in shoals', she reported that: 'I blandly told them to drink wine & have a room of their own.'

The very phrase *A Room of One's Own* has made its way into the annals of feminism – and yet it is a slim volume, written in a lively and often fictitious style, in which Virginia propounds the notion that in order to write fiction a woman must have £500 a year (i.e. decent private means) and a room of her own. The narrator begins by describing her visit to an Oxbridge college, where she is denied access to the library because of her sex, and where, moreover, her luxurious lunch as a guest at a men's college contrasts with the plain fare on offer at a women's college. 'Why should all the splendour, all the luxury of life be lavished on the Julians and the Francises', she asked her diary on returning from Girton.

From there Virginia moved on to some of the questions that had informed both her literature and her life. How was a woman writer to avoid the insidious whisper of the 'Angel in the House', how was it that women had served for centuries as looking glasses 'reflecting the figure of man at twice his natural size'? How could women – or 'woman' – be so ubiquitous in poetry, and yet so absent in history? Had Shakespeare had a sister, what forces might have inhibited her from writing plays?

Virginia was speaking in the year 1928. British women had gained the right to vote on the same terms as men (as opposed to the partial franchise they had won a decade earlier). It was the year Marguerite Radclyffe Hall's lesbian novel *The Well of Loneliness* was tried for, and found guilty of, obscenity, a case in which both Virginia and Vita were deeply interested. Yet in this climate she was promoting

Virginia photographed by Duncan Grant in the early 1930s, gazing out of a window.

the idea of a new fiction that might explore how 'Chloe likes Olivia'. 'I shall be attacked for a feminist and hinted at for a Sapphist', she prophesied before *A Room of One's Own* came out.

Vita's review suggested that Virginia was 'too sensible to be a thorough-going feminist', but some of the ideas in the book were surely those proved by Vita herself. As Virginia put it: in every human being 'a vacillation from one sex to the other takes place', as, of course, it had in *Orlando*. She believed that it was 'fatal to be a man or woman pure and simple; one must be woman-manly or man-womanly. There had to be some collaboration in the mind, some marriage of opposites between the woman and the man, for the art of creation to succeed.

Vita and Harold were speaking publicly on the same theme. Harold was on the point of resigning from the diplomatic service – Vita's hatred of the life, when she visited him in Berlin, had convinced him it was incompatible with his marriage. In their

Vita emphatically disagreed with Harold's suggestion that 'the joys of motherhood' were enough to compensate for the loss of a career.

June 1929 joint radio broadcast on 'Marriage', they agreed that marriage was a living organism, 'a plant not a piece of furniture'. Harold, provocative but with an element of badinage, claimed that 'the most virile woman is infinitely more feminine than the most effeminate man'; Vita emphatically disagreed with his suggestion that 'the joys of motherhood' were enough to compensate for the loss of a career. Why should it always be the woman 'who surrenders her opportunity to her duty'? Their subject was all the more ironic for the fact that Vita was now having an affair with the BBC's Director of Talks, Hilda Matheson.

Hilda was a source of some dispute between Vita and Virginia. Two months after the talk, Virginia's diary admitted that she was cross with Vita, who hadn't told her until the last minute that she was going abroad with Hilda. 'Lord Lord! I am half amused though: why do I mind? What do I mind? How much do I mind?' It was half fun – 'I shall fire up and accuse her' – and half fastidiousness.

Virginia 'like the damned intellectual snob I am' hated to be in any way linked with Hilda and her 'earnest aspiring competent wooden face'. She detested what she called the '2ndrate schoolgirl atmosphere' in which women like Hilda and Dorothy Wellesley enveloped Vita. She was uneasy with Vita's lesbian circles – like the trio centring around Ellen Terry's daughter Edy Craig at Smallhythe Place, near Vita's base in the Weald of Kent – preferring to be an observer of this as of every other scene.

The composer and former suffragette Dame Ethel Smyth had a romantic adoration for Virginia. She compared getting to know her to the thrill of first hearing the music of Brahms.

Harold's return home meant less intensity in the relationship of the two women. By the same token in July 1930 Virginia was returning from a night at Long Barn, where she had been rambling over the new fields Vita had bought, but found herself 'all of a quiver with homecoming to L[eonard].' 'I daresay few women are happier ... It has not been dull – my marriage; not at all.'

That year had brought a new influence into Virginia's life, when she met the composer (and former militant suffragette) Dame Ethel Smyth. A 'bluff, military old woman' was how Virginia initially described her, 'a little glazed flyaway & abrupt', but discriminating. Ethel, most of whose romances had been with women, made no secret of her feelings for Virginia, who noted complacently that she got two letters a day from her. 'I daresay the old fires of Sapphism are blazing for the

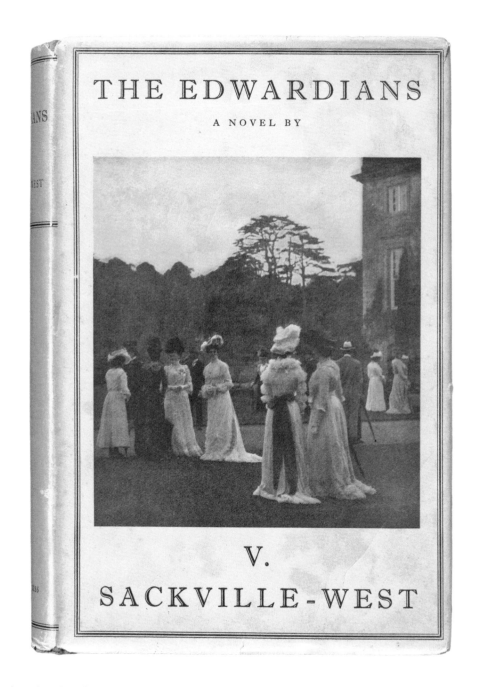

The Edwardians began as a joke, an answer to Orlando. But in the end Vita could not resist celebrating the life of great Edwardian country houses.

last time.' Smyth was now in her seventies. 'But dear me I am not in love with Ethel.' Virginia, while sometimes irritated by Ethel, was nonetheless prepared to take advantage of Ethel's friendship, as Ethel gave her full permission to do. 'The other night, sitting on the floor by my side, Vita suffered considerably from jealousy of Ethel. She praised her, stoutly, but bitterly.'

Vita had recently achieved a measure of reconciliation with her mother, who, early in 1930, even gave Vita back the famous pearls. That year Vita brought out *The Edwardians*, a novel in many ways about her own family. The great country house in which it is set, 'Chevron', is easily identifiable as Knole, and the daily life of the Edwardian upper class is chronicled with the intimacy of one who had lived it; the waste and the extravagance, as Vita wrote to Virginia, 'the sleepy maids waiting about after dinner in the passages'. 'No character in this book is wholly fictitious', Vita wrote in her Author's Note. It was not a goodbye to her past – Knole would not be set aside so easily – but it was perhaps an *au revoir*.

It was also a bestseller. Virginia wrote – in an echo of her childhood in the fishing village of St Ives – that she and Leonard, as the book's publishers, were hauling in money 'like pilchards from a net'. *Orlando* too had been a financial success: in June 1929 Virginia noted that she had in the last half-year made £1,800, almost the salary of a Cabinet minister. Two years before, she had struggled to make £200. She was becoming more famous – profiles of her were published, lectures were sought. But, she had told her diary in March, 'I am going to enter a nunnery these next months: & let myself down into my mind; Bloomsbury being done with. I am going to face certain things. It is going to be a time of adventure & attack, rather lonely & painful I think.'

Virginia felt, she wrote, 'on the verge of some strenuous adventure'. Would it be one in which Vita had a major part? They continued to meet on a regular basis – little expeditions in London, to the Tower, the zoo, 'or to eat muffins in a shop'. But Vita too was setting out on her own lone adventure. It was one that would divide her from her friend, though one in which Harold, unlike Virginia, would have an important if subsidiary share.

Sissinghurst

Not the least significant event, as the 1920s gave way to a new decade, was an unwelcome piece of local, country news that came to the Nicolsons. The farm adjacent to Long Barn was being bought by poultry farmers, who were planning to erect cottages and chicken huts overlooking their garden. Ironically – in the light of future developments – it was Vita who was the more reluctant to move. But an unexpected find changed her mind, and on 4 April 1930 she telephoned Harold to say she had found them 'the ideal house'. Sissinghurst Castle had been on the market for two years, which was hardly surprising, since only the wreckage remained of the once-great Elizabethan house.

Two derelict cottages, an entrance arch, farm buildings and a brick tower – stripped of its original surrounds – like something from a fairy story. Or 'like a bewitched and rosy fountain', as Vita said, pointing towards the sky. Her mother had said long ago that all Vita wanted was to live alone in a tower with her books. Now she could make the dream come true.

'Lovely pink brick; but like Knole, not much view, save of stables', Virginia would coolly note when she saw the tower, two years later. But there was nothing cool about Vita's own response. She had fallen 'flat in love'.

But her thirteen-year-old son Nigel, who came with her, was appalled. Where were they going to live, he asked, since 'not a single room was habitable'? No water laid on, no electricity, with the roofs fallen in. Trailing from one brick fragment to another, in the rain, between mountains of old bedsteads, sardine tins and cabbage stalks, he was aghast when his mother turned to him and said: 'I think we shall be very happy here.' She thought they could make 'something very lovely' out of it.

The orchard was always intended as a kind of wilderness, with spring bulbs planted under the fruit trees, and the remains of the original house buried under the grass.

Above: The gazebo over the moat was built by Nigel Nicolson in memory of his father Harold.
Following pages: Among the charms of Sissinghurst are its lovely views over the Weald of Kent.

In the remnants of the great Elizabethan house, Vita saw the ghost of Knole. Sissinghurst Castle had once been a mansion of three great courts, adapted from medieval origins into the most luxurious Tudor style, surrounded by parkland, and grand enough to have hosted, in 1573, Elizabeth I and her court. Those days were long gone, but perhaps, even, the very ruination of the Sissinghurst she now saw made a visceral appeal to Vita. 'It was Sleeping Beauty's Castle; but a castle running away into sordidness and squalor; a garden crying out for rescue.'

Vita always saw Knole, in the hands of its new owners, as being damaged, broken, destroyed. Knole in its physical form was lost to her, even though Virginia had done something to give its spirit back. But Sissinghurst was different. Sissinghurst she could save.

Driving there in the spring, the season of blossom, through the county called the Garden of England, she had seen the England she feared was vanishing and had written of in *The Land*. Now she found another link with the past. In the mid-sixteenth century, Sissinghurst had been owned by the rising man John Baker, whose daughter Cecily married Thomas Sackville, first Earl of Dorset, the man to whom Elizabeth I had given Knole.

It made the ruin feel like a family home. And it was Vita's family money that bought it – Harold would never legally have a share in the property. The flag eventually flying over the tower would bear her family crest, even the garden tools would all be stamped with 'V.S-W'. Vita would tell her son Ben that the roots one found in one's own home were the deepest of all, and this would be where her roots could spread.

Not that Harold was against the purchase, though daunted by the challenge it posed. The day after Vita and Nigel had seen it, he went down with their other son Ben. 'I am cold and calm but I like it.' A few weeks later, with the purchase still under discussion, he wrote to Vita, 'a) That it is most unwise of us to get Sissinghurst.' For the same money, more than £12,000 to buy and another good £15,000 to put in order, they could get a beautiful finished property. 'b) That it is most wise of us to buy Sissinghurst.' He noted – in what was sure to be a potent appeal to Vita – that 'through its veins pulses the blood of the Sackville dynasty.' It was in Kent, they both liked it … the deal was done, basically.

Like Vita, he was prepared to overlook its eccentricities as a living space. Indeed in the years ahead he would describe it as 'the strangest conglomeration of shapeless buildings that you ever saw, but it is an affectionate house and very mellow and English'. The Sissinghurst estate comprised also a spacious ten-bedroom Victorian farmhouse but, to the puzzlement of the estate agents, Vita never considered living in that.

At first, Vita and Harold considered building extensions to link the surviving brick buildings one to another, but soon changed their minds, and not just from lack of money. On one side of the gatehouse would be staff accommodation; on the other, what had been the stables would become a long library-cum-sitting room, large enough to take the portraits of Vita's ancestors and the one Philip de László had painted of her as a girl. Harold and Vita themselves would have bedrooms, and he a study, in what is now known as the South Cottage. The boys would be housed in the Priest's House, as would the family kitchen and dining room, which meant a walk across the garden, several times a day, in all weathers and often in the dark.

But Harold would later write to Vita that: 'I have often wondered what makes the perfect family, I think it is just our compound of intimacy and aloofness. Each of us has

a room of his own. Each of us knows that there is a common-room where we meet on the basis of perfect understanding.' Sissinghurst would be the brick embodiment of that ideal.

There was, however, a daunting amount of work to be done before the dwellings were habitable. Sissinghurst had gone through several periods of despoliation in its history. The decline from its Tudor heyday had begun in the seventeenth century when there had been no male heir to the Baker line. For years the house lay empty, so that Horace Walpole, passing by in 1749, found 'a park in ruins and a house in ten times greater ruins.'

Worse was shortly to follow, when it was rented out as a prison for as many as 3,000 captured French seamen during the Seven Years' War. Conditions were appalling – Sissinghurst was the prison with which prisoners elsewhere were threatened if they misbehaved – and the brutalised Frenchmen vented their fury on the house and garden. When they left, 2,000ft (610m) of glass and 200ft (61m) of wainscot had been destroyed, 'and not even the rump of a shrub or tree left'. As a parish poorhouse was set up in the stables, cows grazed the courtyards where Elizabethan courtiers had walked.

It would be two years before the family could live there full time, and the garden, of course, would take much, much longer.

Rescue of a kind came when, for the second half of the nineteenth century, the farm of Sissinghurst was rented out to dynamic and successful tenants. Hops and cereal crops were planted, fields drained and cattle bred. The family, however, conducted operations from the new Victorian farmhouse, and the Sissinghurst Castle Estate, in 21 lots, was sold again in 1903. Any thought of restoring the Castle itself failed in the light of the agricultural depression that struck the new century.

Vita and Harold's first nights in their new home were spent camped out in the chill of the tower. It would be two years before the family could live there full time, and the garden, of course, would take much, much longer. The labourers who occupied Sissinghurst in the last phase of the house's history had left the garden as 'a dump', Vita wrote later, for rusty iron and used it as a run for chickens, the rubbish muddled up in a tangle of bindweed and nettles. Clearing the refuse alone would take three years – but that was only the start. This was a work not of restoration, but of creation. With only one flowering plant left as reminder of any former garden – the rampant *Rosa gallica* later dubbed 'Sissinghurst Castle' – they were starting virtually from scratch.

The South Cottage was where Vita and Harold had their bedrooms, with Harold's book room and their private sitting room.

From the start the garden was conceived as a series of smaller enclosures – each different, each a new discovery – around a double axis. The designing brain was that of Harold, who, Vita boasted proudly, 'should have been a garden-architect in another life.' She, however, was the plantswoman. She knew by instinct that there should be 'the strictest formality of design, with the maximum of informality in planting. The rosy walls might not run straight, but they cried out for a tumble of Roses and Honeysuckles, Figs and Vines.' Indeed, on the very day of purchase they planted a climbing rose against the walls of the South Cottage, 'Mme Alfred Carrière'.

One of the few traces of the old garden Vita and Harold had found when they first saw the property was a nuttery, a plantation of Kentish cobnuts. They had taken the discovery as a sign that a garden could grow here again, and now planted a carpet of polyanthus under the trees with narcissi and foxgloves, which Harold carted from the woods in an old pram. They commissioned the clearing of the Moat Walk, the damming of a stream to make a lake, and the planting of a row of yews to separate the Tower Lawn from the orchard.

'All is planned', Virginia wrote when the Woolfs visited just two years after the purchase. 'H[arold] has drawn it in his note book. Walls have been built & turf laid.' In fact all was far from planned — it would be two decades before the creation of the White Garden, which became Sissinghurst's most famous feature. Some of Harold's more grandiose ideas would be abandoned, and even his designs for the kitchen garden were temporarily thwarted by 'artichokes and Vita's indignation'.

Vita herself would say later that she knew nothing about gardening in 1930, that she 'planted all the wrong things and planted them in the wrong places.' But perhaps that very readiness to replan and to replant where necessary — to learn from the lie of the land, and let the garden develop down the decades — would help to make Sissinghurst one of the best-loved names in English garden history.

Above: Vita and Harold utilised all surviving fragments of the once-great Tudor house. The front range and entrance arch were probably built in the 1530s. Opposite: The Cottage Garden outside the South Cottage is ablaze with hot colour, at its best towards the end of summer. It could be seen from Harold's writing desk, and from Vita's bedroom.

PART III

1931–62
All Passion Spent

The partnership of Vita and Harold only deepened as the years wore on, and although she spent far more time at Sissinghurst, work there – on the garden, and on their books – would continue to be a strong tie between them.

CHAPTER 6

⋮ 1931–8 ⋮

I n 1931 Vita and Harold's marriage had still more than half its length to run. There was, wrote their son Nigel, 'no change in their relationship from that time forward, no threat to their married happiness. It simply deepened.' Vita herself would write to Harold some years later how remarkable it was that, with their sons heading towards 30, 'I should love you so much more than I did when we made them.' Then she had been very much in love, she wrote, but it been like a mountain spring while 'now it is like a deep deep lake which can never dry up.'

Both would continue to have affairs. As Harold told his diary: 'I have got into the way of taking my happiness for granted.' Yet Vita was 'not a person one can take for granted.' And a letter Virginia wrote to Vita shortly acknowledged – or was it more a complaint? – that 'you know you love now several people, women I mean, better, oftener, more carnally than me.' She described Vita once as falling in love with every pretty woman 'just like a man'. Vita's active sexual career saw her the lover of perhaps as many as 50 women with, often repeated, her mother's pattern of wilfulness; an emotional dependency she provoked but was then unwilling or unable to satisfy.

Yet Vita had told Virginia a few years earlier that as she got older, she found herself more and more 'disagreeably solitary', going so far into herself there was a danger she would become quite lost. Then, she said she relied on Virginia to pull off the covers from time to time. Now, in 1931, Vita (and the Hogarth Press) brought out the poem *Sissinghurst*, dedicated to 'VW', in which Vita pictured herself as 'water-drowned', seeking silence, sinking voluntarily beneath the waters of a stagnant moat.

As Vita burrowed down into Sissinghurst, Harold was finding it ever harder to bear being cut off from her for long periods at a time. Since leaving the Foreign Office he'd joined the staff of the *Evening Standard*, working also for the *Daily Express* and for the BBC, where he became famous for his weekly talks, *People and Things*. But his life was still one of house parties with Churchill (recorded as going on a long walk with Vita) and lunches at Chequers. Politics was the obvious next step. He joined Oswald Mosley's New Party in the teeth of Vita's disbelief, but began to split with them as the New Party was subsumed into the British Union of Fascists, a movement with which he could not agree.

Their shortage of money troubled Harold more than Vita. Many of the early plans for the buildings of Sissinghurst were abandoned, though not always for motives of cost. All the same they were happy, as he told his diary: 'all this uncertainty is better for us than a dull and unadventurous security.' As he began to write – a novel, as well as more political volumes – they felt they could celebrate 'a lovely year'.

Vita and Virginia continued to meet on a regular basis, but Sissinghurst had no guest rooms, and Virginia only ever spent one night there, staying in Harold's bedroom. 'My dear, remote, romantic Virginia …' wrote Vita from Sissinghurst once, to a Virginia sliding down the Dalmatian coastline.

Yet only months before it had been Virginia pathetically asking Ethel Smyth whether Vita (now in the throes of a passionate affair with Evelyn Irons, the Women's Page editor of the *Daily Mail*, and involved simultaneously with Evelyn's

On first meeting Vita – photographed here at Monk's House – Virginia described her as 'florid, moustached, parakeet coloured'.

lover Olive Rinder) '*really* wants me in her life?' In a way, Ethel wrote to Vita – both generously and perceptively – Virginia was 'on the rim of everyone's life … that the human contact others can achieve is not for such as her … And so I wanted you to turn on the human tap somehow – anyhow I felt she wanted to be reassured'. Virginia herself had already written to Ethel that she was 'one of the kindest of women … with that maternal quality which of all others I need and adore.' The quality she had once noted in Vita.

The new decade had begun for Virginia, in the cold early spring of 1930, with one of those illnesses she had come to feel were 'partly mystical'. Part, that is, of her process as a writer. 'Something happens in my mind. It refuses to go on registering impressions. It shuts itself up. It becomes chrysalis. I lie quite torpid, often with acute physical pain … Then suddenly something springs.' As it had done two days before, when Vita was there.

But Virginia had come to the same basic decision as Vita: her husband Leonard was and would remain her 'inviolable centre', as well as her most honest critic. In 1931 (as Vita published the popular *All Passion Spent*, in which the widowed elderly Lady Slane finally takes control of her own life and her own pleasure), Virginia completed and brought out *The Waves*, the book she had originally imagined as 'a mind thinking' and perhaps her most experimental novel – what she described as 'prose yet poetry; a novel & a play', and also as autobiography. The first draft alone had taken her almost two years. It consisted of soliloquies from six characters, who however, Virginia wrote, 'were supposed to be one. I'm getting old myself … and I come to feel more and more how difficult it is to collect oneself into one Virginia'.

Virginia recorded, not without relish, that no two people felt the same about the book. Vita thought it 'so bad that only a small dog that had been fed on gin could have written it.' But Leonard told her it was a masterpiece (though doubting the 'common reader' would manage to follow the first 100 pages). When Harold phoned to add his praise it left her 'trembling with pleasure'. E.M. Forster wrote to her of its importance – and in fact Leonard would prove to have been pessimistic: common readers, as she recorded in her diary, rushed to buy this book more eagerly than any other.

> *The new decade had begun for Virginia, in the cold early spring of 1930, with one of those illnesses she had come to feel were 'partly mystical'.*

Leonard's spaniel Sally, painted by Vanessa Bell. Virginia noted her fine domed head and bloodhound's muzzle, and that they had paid £18 for her.

'Oh yes, between 50 and 60' – she told her diary in November 1931, two months before her fiftieth birthday – 'I think I shall write out some very singular books, if I live. I mean I think I am about to embody at last the exact shapes my brain holds.' *The Waves* might be 'my first work in my own style.'

A year later, she was still reflecting this new mood that had come to her with her fifties: 'I don't believe in ageing. I believe in forever altering one's aspect to the sun. Hence my optimism.' She was breaching some new frontiers, writing an introduction to *Life As We Have Known It*, a collection of memoirs by members of the Women's Co-operative Guild – a plate-layer's wife, a hat-maker, a former servant. Perhaps it did something to bridge the gap for which she is often criticised, but which she herself acknowledged, between her experience and that of working-class women.

Though Virginia would in these years turn down a number of public honours – an honorary doctorate, the chance to be made a Companion of Honour, an invitation to deliver a series of prestigious lectures at Cambridge – she was increasingly feeling the need to have a public voice. In 1931 she and Ethel Smyth had appeared on a platform together for what would later be named the Fawcett Society, founded 'to obtain economic equality for women'. The speech she had made there would lead, some years on, to her book *Three Guineas*, more explicitly feminist than *A Room of One's Own*. Speaking on 'Professions for Women', she listed 'makers of scientific models, accountants, hospital dieticians, political organisers, store keepers, artists, horticultural instructors, publicity managers, architects …' In the months afterwards, she began to keep a file of press cuttings displaying sexual prejudice and double standards until, she said, by 1932, she had 'enough powder to blow up St Paul's.'

She was, by the early 1930s, increasingly engaging in debate with a new generation of writers – Stephen Spender, Christopher Isherwood, C. Day-Lewis. These young men – coming into her orbit partly through John Lehmann (brother of the novelist Rosamond Lehmann) who had joined the Hogarth Press – were eager to engage with the working man, instinctively hostile towards privileged cliques. They simultaneously rejected and were indebted to the Bloomsbury world. Virginia's feelings towards them were as complex. But then 1931 – a year of economic crisis, in the wake of the American stock market crash, and the year of the collapse of Britain's minority Labour government – was a year of intense political debate, in which Leonard was directly involved. Europe was in the grip of the Depression, with – almost a decade after Mussolini came to power in Italy – Hitler now rising in Germany also. Virginia saw only 'idiotic, meaningless, brutal, bloody, pandemonium' ahead.

In this climate Virginia's next novel, *Flush* – a slight volume couched as a biography of Elizabeth Barrett Browning's spaniel – might have seemed a mere *jeu d'esprit*. But it was a huge bestseller at the time, and more recently it has been seen as a political or a feminist narrative, or even as an allegory of her affair with Vita – who had given her the spaniel whose image provided the book's frontispiece. Before that book came out Virginia was already complaining that the public interest in her own life was too much for her – 'limelight is bad for me: the light in which I work best is twilight. And I'm threatened with 3 more books upon me … a kind of fuss and falsity and talking about my husband, mother, father, and dog which I loathe'. Even Harold Nicolson had been broadcasting on her, bracketing her with T.S. Eliot, D.H. Lawrence, James Joyce and Evelyn Waugh as a 'modernist', though Woolf complained it was a 'crime and a scandal' to divide up the writers of the age that way.

One great shadow, however, was the death, in January 1932, of Lytton Strachey from stomach cancer. He had in a sense epitomised Bloomsbury, and his passing further weakened the ties of a Bloomsbury Group already drifting apart. It also made Virginia feel old. Dora Carrington, the young artist who had long loved and set up house with the homosexual Strachey, wrote to Virginia that her letters had been most use of all, 'because you understand'. (Virginia for her part had told Vita she should mind it to the end of her days if Lytton died. It would be 'like having the globe of the future perpetually smashed.') In March she visited Carrington, praising how much she had given Lytton, holding her small hands, and hating, she wrote, to leave her alone. The next day, Carrington shot herself. Virginia's reaction was one of protest. 'I am glad to be alive and sorry for the dead; can't think why Carrington killed herself & put an end to all this.'

In 1933 Vita shared with Virginia her distress over her mother having taken it upon herself to tell her elder son Ben about Vita and Virginia's 'morals' – 'Not that I am in any way ashamed … Only Ben might have had a horrid imprint sealed on his mind.' They still sought to dine with each other 'alone' – still sought to see each other in sickness and in health. Virginia wrote to Vita only half mockingly, on hearing Vita had been seen lunching at the Café Royal – 'yes and it was a woman you were lunching with, and there was I sitting alone, and and and …' Vita replied in her playful identity of 'a rather shabby sheepdog', which merely gnawed its bone at the Café.

But as so often, Virginia's diaries show her looking at Vita with a colder eye than in her letters. In July 1934 she noted that Vita had come to lunch after many weeks, bringing the manuscript of her controversial novel *The Dark Island*, featuring a sadistic three-way relationship. 'She has grown opulent & bold & red – underneath much the same; only without the porpoise radiance, & the pearls lost lustre.' Virginia noted disapprovingly that Vita now painted her fingers and lips – 'the influence of Gwen'.

In the summer of 1933, Gwen St Aubyn, Harold Nicolson's younger sister, had come to Sissinghurst to convalesce after a terrible car accident. It was Gwen who led Vita towards a fashionable interest in mysticism and the occult. Even Katherine Mansfield in her last days had become a follower of the mystic Gurdjieff. The pursuit offered a rationale for Vita's own mounting desire for solitude and offered, too, a framework in which a number of female (and lesbian) writers were re-examining the lives of the female saints. Perhaps it was inevitable that Vita the former tomboy should choose for the subject of her next book the cross-dressing Joan of Arc. Vita's strong personal relationship with Gwen also featured in *The Dark Island*.

Virginia was deeply shocked in September of 1934 by the unexpected death of Roger Fry, from heart failure after a fall. (By contrast the death of George Duckworth, that April, had seen her elegaic and surprisingly affectionate: 'Poor old creature … How childhood goes with him.') But more had gone from life with the loss of Roger's 'large sweet soul'. By the end of the year, moreover, Virginia had been asked by Roger's sister and his lover to write his biography, a task she would find much more wearing than she anticipated.

On visits to Sissinghurst and elsewhere, Virginia developed her own relationship with Vita's growing sons, Ben and Nigel. Nigel remembered her as fun and easy company – 'delicate, but in the cobweb sense, not the medical.' He would later edit six volumes of Virginia's *Letters*.

The following spring, after a visit to a cold and windy Sissinghurst, Virginia was more unsympathetic than ever to Vita's preoccupation with the place.

Her friendship with Vita was over, she wrote in her diary. 'Not with a quarrel, not with a bang, but as a ripe fruit falls.' Vita's voice calling her name still had the power to thrill, but then disillusionment set in. 'And she has grown very fat, very much the indolent country lady, run to seed, incurious now about books; has

Virginia originally conceived *The Years* as a 'novel-essay' in which to explore her ideas about the social position of women.

written no poetry; only kindles about dogs, flowers, & new buildings.'

There was, she said 'no bitterness, & no disillusion, only a certain emptiness', and perhaps that was partly a reflection of her own rather barren state of mind after what she saw as Vita's 'defection'. But Virginia's prediction that 'there's an end to it' would not prove entirely true. Indeed, five months later, back at Sissinghurst, she noted: 'Saw the great new room. Vita in trousers. Rather woke my affection & regret.'

Vita was indeed ever more the country dweller. When at the end of 1935 Harold agreed to stand for Parliament, contesting and winning the Leicester West seat as a National Labour candidate, Vita – very sorry, she wrote, to hurt him, but sticking to their old agreement – refused to appear at any of his functions or platforms; something that caused even the long-suffering Hadji to complain she had never taken any interest in what mattered to him. A letter of hers admitted that 'I do feel so dull always, compared with your life' – that she must seem 'dull and rustic' to him. But she had made her choice.

Harold, it is true, was living at a colourful and elevated level. Passing through Paris took him to James Joyce's flat, a trip to America saw Ben taken flying by Charles Lindbergh. In London he dined with the Prince of Wales and Wallis Simpson – 'bejewelled, eyebrow-plucked, virtuous and wise' – and bumped into 'a dear little patapouf in black' who belatedly he realised was the Duchess of York, the future Queen Mother.

Vita too was not altogether the country bumpkin. In February 1934 letters exchanged with Virginia show her (to Virginia's amusement) in Marrakesh with the Princess Royal and Lord Lascelles, who had once been her own suitor. (Vita noted that she had seen a European edition of *Orlando* even there.) In January 1936

Vita's mother died: Vita felt she had been 'hit over the head with a mallet', but it was a break with the past, and in some ways a positive one. Harold thought she was 'much harassed and shattered, but inwardly, I think, relieved.' Certainly their financial life would now be considerably easier. The following year Vita would bring out a biography of her grandmother, Pepita, and work on it allowed her to look back on her mother Victoria, too, seeing her with 'all the silly little irritations fading and the real quality emerging.'

Sissinghurst united rather than divided Vita and Harold. 'I do so love the garden' he wrote to her on 13 May 1936. 'It is a sort of still backcloth to my rattley ruttley rottley … life.' He was on the rise – Vice-Chairman of the Foreign Affairs Committee. But the foreign situation could only be cause for the very deepest concern. In 1937 it was brought most painfully home to Virginia when Vanessa's son Julian Bell, who had gone to drive an ambulance on the Republican side in the Spanish Civil War, was killed after barely a month. Vanessa told Vita what a comfort Virginia had been to her; Virginia praised Vita's (and Harold's) 'silent goodness' after a visit to Sissinghurst. But Virginia found that her daily visits to Nessa, her support in the face of Nessa's despair, was 'very hard work'.

At the point of Julian's death Virginia had already been on something of a roller coaster. In the spring of 1936, after two months' dismal and almost catastrophic illness, she had 'never been so near the precipice to my own feeling since 1913'. 'Now I'm again on top … Oh but the divine joy of being mistress of my mind again!' She had been editing *The Years* and feared being greeted by 'a roar of laughter at my expense' on publication of the book. More conventional in form than her recent work, this was the chronicle of a middle-class family over some 50 years, albeit in a series of seemingly random moments which evaded conventional ideas of plot or action. ('It's the thing we do in the dark that is more real.') Contrary to Virginia's fears it was another commercial success, but she continued to see it as an 'odious rice pudding of a book'.

In November 1937 Vita sent a letter 'from the pink tower' of Sissinghurst lamenting that other people – even Vita's cousin Eddy – had seen Virginia but she had not. Did Virginia ever think of her? A 'thought of love from your *Orlando*'. She always turned to Virginia, she wrote, when she felt 'like the dustbin with fireworks inside it'.

Virginia wrote back reassuringly, why such doubt? 'Just because you choose to sit in the mud in Kent and I on the flags of London, that's no reason why love should fade is it? Why the pearls and the porpoise should vanish …' It sounds as though they were still feeling their way into a new aspect of their relationship. Their letters breathe anxieties, along with, or allied to, their affection. When Vita is ill and rushed to hospital in London she doesn't tell Virginia; Vita simultaneously apologises for not writing, and enthuses over the idea of a meeting in a way that does not quite ring true.

Through the 1930s Virginia had been supporting Leonard's work for the Labour Party and even taking on her own work for anti-war causes, albeit with a dislike for political institutions that left her making as many gestures of withdrawal as of commitment. She was a member of a number of anti-Fascist organisations, sitting on a number of committees, lending her support to campaigns to get a pacifist writer out of a concentration camp and to get Picasso's *Guernica* on display in Britain. She complained however that Leonard's frenzied activity after Hitler invaded the Rhineland in March 1936 had left her feeling like 'the charwoman of a Prime Minister'.

All Bloomsbury was deeply perturbed by the threat to personal and intellectual liberty they saw, rightly, as posed by the Nazi Party. But they would be divided between those who having lived through the First World War maintained a determined pacifism in the Second, and those who felt this threat so great there was no avoiding the fight. It would indeed even cause a measure of division between the Woolfs: Rose Macaulay wrote that 'She is for Peace, Leonard for the war.'

Virginia's husband would later describe her as 'the least political animal that has lived' – an aspect of the persistent image of her as a fey, unworldly creature – though later generations of critics and biographers would not always agree. But Virginia's writing, at least, was becoming more directly political – in the face of the war threat, she was, as a writer, inclined to move away from fiction. The alienation of women from the male-dominated sphere of politics and public activity was in a sense the theme of her next book *Three Guineas*, which drew a parallel between a world moving towards war and a world of women subject to the domination of the patriarchy. 'Are they not both the voices of Dictators, whether they speak English or German?' 'All the gents against me', she would note, after a discussion as to whether a fresh war really represented the end of civilisation.

In the summer of 1938 Virginia sent Vita a copy of the new *Three Guineas*. Virginia had always known the book would be divisive, and in many ways relished the fact. But there was a sense of being with her or against her, and when Vita complained of the book's 'misleading arguments', Virginia took sharp exception. Both women drew in their horns – 'So forgive and forget', Virginia said. Vita's

Finding the Nuttery at Sissinghurst helped Vita and Harold decide on the property. Ferns, white bluebells and euphorbia now foam under the plantation of Kentish cobnuts. In Vita's day it was a brilliant carpet of polyanthus.

poem *Solitude*, published by the Hogarth Press in 1938, seems to contrast other 'cheap and easy loves' with what she and Virginia shared. She still considered Virginia 'very beautiful indeed in your brown fur cap and your exquisitely ethereal slenderness.'

All the same, for Virginia, *Three Guineas*, with its suggestion of a 'Society of Outsiders', represented, as she put it, the throwing aside of a cloak. She felt she was now no longer famous, no longer on a pedestal, 'on my own, forever'. She had had her say, 'take it or leave it', had committed herself and was afraid of nothing. A sense of freedom, of putting slippers on – 'free for fresh adventure – at the age of 56'. She had sold to John Lehmann her half of the Hogarth Press and hoped to relish the removal of that care as much as the money she was now making. But her long-running biography of Roger Fry was causing endless problems. Hoping to fly free, to invent a new form of biography, she found herself instead drowning in a sea of facts and research materials, constrained by the censorship of his family. And there was no avoiding the political situation. Virginia to her diary in August 1938: 'A single step – in Czechoslovakia – like the Austrian archduke in 1914 – and again

it's 1914. Ding dong ding dong.' She described to Vanessa a London of sandbags in the streets, of the doling out of gas masks.

In September, with Neville Chamberlain's 'peace for our time' speech, it all seemed to go away, but Harold Nicolson – quietly, but with utter commitment, anti-appeasement – was one person who could guess it was only a temporary respite.

Sissinghurst still helped – planting lupins, seeing how the new willows were coming on. They were beginning to open the garden to the public on occasion, for charity, and the Sissinghurst style was beginning to make its way into gardening history. But on 9 April 1939, as Harold and Vita were planting annuals in the cottage garden, in the border and in the orchard. 'We rake the soil smooth. And as we rake we are both thinking, "What will have happened to the world when these seeds germinate? It is warm and still."' Virginia wrote that all the country 'was thinking the same thing – the horror of war – at the same moment.'

On 29 August Virginia wrote to Vita from Rodmell, 'another day of peace – gardening, playing bowls, listening to the radio and cooking.' The day before, she had told her diary: 'Vita says she feels terror & horror early – revives then sinks. For us it's like being on a small island' – a 'vast cold gloom', and the strain as of a doctor's waiting room. 'We privately are so content. Bliss day after day … How to go on, through war? – that's the question.'

Private difficulties compounded the public ones. In August the Woolfs moved from Tavistock Square, whose lease was up after fifteen years, to 37 Mecklenburgh Square. In that spring Virginia had begun writing her *Sketch of the Past* which perhaps reopened wounds, about the feelings, so 'dumb and mixed' she hardly knew how to describe them, provoked by Gerald's abuse, by her relationship with Thoby.

On 1 September 1939 Harold was sitting in a deckchair at the door of the South Cottage, with fuchsias and zinnias and yellow butterflies before his eyes but one ear cocked for the telephone, when he saw Vita coming through the cottage garden. 'It has begun,' she said.

As the political situation darkened, towards the end of the 1930s Sissinghurst's fruitful beauty came to seem like a refuge.

CHAPTER 7

⋮ 1939–43 ⋮

It would in fact be two more days before, on 3 September 1939, war was declared. Even then, Harold, walking down to bathe in the lake at Sissinghurst, found himself amazed at the indifference of the swans. But this was the so-called Phoney War, the eight-month pause before the start of Britain's real involvement in hostilities. In May 1940 – as Winston Churchill took office, replacing a discredited Neville Chamberlain – Harold would be appointed Parliamentary Secretary to the Ministry of Information, responsible for coordinating government advice to the public in case of an invasion, which looked all too likely.

The Nicolsons had discussed whether defeat was a possibility and if so whether to 'surrender in advance' – suicide – would not be the better option. On 26 May Harold wrote to Vita urging her, in case the Germans invaded and occupied Sissinghurst, to have a 'bare bodkin' handy 'so that you can take your quietus when necessary. I shall have one also.' He said he would ask his doctor friend for advice – and did indeed obtain a lethal pill for suicide in case of capture.

The Woolfs similarly acquired a lethal dose of morphia from Adrian Stephen, now a psychiatric army doctor, and Leonard had petrol stored in the garage with which to gas themselves. Leonard and Virginia could not know that both their names were in Hitler's 'Black Book', but Leonard was of course a Jew.

Virginia had told her diary on the outbreak of war that this was the worst of all her life's experiences – 'all creative power is cut off.'

Virginia, she said, still did not want 'to go to bed at midday'. But she had told her diary on the outbreak of war that this was the worst of all her life's experiences – 'all creative power is cut off.' To her niece Angelica she wrote that 'rats in caves live as we do'. From the start of the war Virginia was based at Monk's House. Visits to London were only depressing. 'The City has become merely a congerie of houses lived in by people who work. There is no society, no luxury no splendour no gadding & flitting.'

Virginia's bedroom at Monk's House opened directly onto the garden. The tiles around the fireplace were decorated for her by Vanessa and she always kept pencil and paper by the bed to record any thoughts that came to her in the night.

In the months before the war she had met Sigmund Freud, in flight from the Nazi regime. Now she began reading his works and found them 'upsetting', at a time when she was already looking backwards, reconsidering her relationship to her father, for *A Sketch of the Past*. The starkness in Freud, which declared the human race would never rid itself of aggression, seemed to say that she herself would never be free of the fear of descending into madness again.

Her professional life was cause for concern – would the public still be buying books? When it came out in the summer of 1940, *Roger Fry* was greeted with 'complete silence'. It would in the end sell, but there was perhaps a sense that the 'elite' (as *The Spectator* put it) world of Bloomsbury was becoming irrelevant. To some – including Vita's son Benedict, whose career as an art historian had been interrupted for war service, and who now wrote to Virginia – this seemed the portrait of a man who had retreated into an ivory tower, taking refuge in

Following pages: Virginia described the Monk's House garden as being 'a perfect variegated chintz' of colour, the flowers 'stiff, upstanding as flowers should be'.

Returning to a bomb-damaged London, Virginia described the mess of ruined buildings and people queueing all day to shelter in Underground stations from the nightly air raids.

his sensibility from the harsher side of life – the same accusation Virginia could imagine being levelled at herself. Another kind of reality had hit home when her maid's brother, one of those who made it off the beaches of Dunkirk, was found lying exhausted outside the door of Monk's House.

She managed to write bracing letters to friends – Vita would get a jokey one in the last days of Virginia's life. But she and Vita, near the south coast, were both beneath the air battles overhead that summer and in the path of invasion that was expected by the autumn of 1940. On the last day of August Virginia's diary describes being on the phone to a Vita she felt could be killed any moment while bombs were falling all around Sissinghurst. 'Can you hear that? she said. No, I couldn't. That's another. That's another. She repeated the same thing – about staying to drive the ambulance – time after time, like a person who can't think.' After putting down the receiver Virginia wrote a letter for Vita that was effectively a farewell: 'You have given me such happiness.'

Virginia at first resisted being photographed by Gisèle Freund, at home in Tavistock Square. She cursed 'this petty vulgar photography-advertising stunt'.

On 11 September Virginia recorded listening to Churchill's speech and realising the invasion 'was for the next two weeks apparently if at all'. The roads were full of lorries, soldiers and machines. Bombs were dropping even in the middle of a bowls game. One came so close she cursed at Leonard, thinking he had slammed a window.

'Oh I try to imagine how one's killed by a bomb', she wrote the following month. The crushing of bone in on her eye and brain, 'a drain; two or three gulps attempting consciousness – and then dot dot dot.'

The Mecklenburgh Square address they had taken over just a year before was bombed in September 1940. They came up to London to find 'dark carpets nailed to windows; ceilings down in patches; heaps of grey dust & china under kitchen table.' A month later it was 52 Tavistock Square. Virginia's diary records her and Leonard's trip to London on 18 October to see 'a heap of ruins … rubble where I wrote so many books. Open air where we sat so many nights, gave so many parties.' A few weeks later they were able to salvage some possessions from Mecklenburgh Square – Virginia's 24 volumes of diaries, plates decorated by Vanessa – wondering what best to cram into their little car. Virginia echoed Leonard's words about the exhilaration of losing possessions, of how peaceful it would be to start life bare and free. But in fact the grimy detritus of their London life just made small, chilly Monk's House even more a 'huddle & hideousness of untidiness'. Rodmell society was never going to be congenial, but now no other was open to her. That cold winter, she and Leonard had not enough fuel to warm her writing room. Virginia no longer had 'A Room of One's Own'.

Someone who met Virginia in these years described her as having the marks of all her dreams imprinted on her face.

Her letters and Vita's had since the start of hostilities been discussing what Vita called their war-psychology. Vita thought Virginia was the braver of the two, or at least the more philosophical about fear … 'I could not write about this to anyone I did not love as I love you.' Virginia responded that she was numbed rather than philosophical. But she found herself in 'a dumb rage, being fought for by these children whom one wants to see making love to each other.' There were, Vita responded, few people these days 'who give me any sense of real contact, but you certainly do.' At the start of the war Vita had visited 'the Wolves' at Rodmell and found Virginia 'well in health, though naturally unhappy in mind', very sweet and affectionate.

Vita's war work lay with the Women's Land Army, about whom she would write a book. But she too was finding life difficult at Sissinghurst, with endless people and 'questions, responsibilities, voices'. The white pigeons 'like magnolia flowers' had flown off, there was no food for her budgerigars. The guards who used the tower for spotting were looking not only for parachutists but for troop-carrying German planes landing on Sissinghurst's very fields. In that terrifying summer of 1940, amid fear of a wholesale civilian evacuation of the southern counties, Harold told Vita to keep the car filled with petrol in readiness to flee.

Vita sent her will and her jewels away to a safer part of the country, and 'the only other treasure I sent was the manuscript of *Orlando*', she told Virginia. The two managed to meet occasionally, despite the rationing of petrol: Virginia's friendship, Vita wrote to her, was still 'one of the major things in my life.' On 10 October 1940 Vita wrote of how much she had enjoyed her visit. 'Darling – thank you for my happy hours with you. You mean more to me than you will ever know.' And Virginia's diary described the same occasion: 'all very ample easy and satisfying … I'm glad that our love has weathered so well.'

But for Vita the first eighteen months of the war was marked also by personal tragedies. In October 1940, Hilda Matheson died after a thyroid operation, throwing Dottie Wellesley (who had turned to Hilda when her relationship with Vita had ended) into incoherent despair. Vita herself had drifted into the habit of drinking too much evening sherry. The following year her son Ben would write to his brother about his mother's 'vicious pleasure' of drunkenness – her 'premature senility'.

Vita sent her will and her jewels away to a safer part of the country, and 'the only other treasure I sent was the manuscript of Orlando'.

As 1940 turned to 1941 Vita also, as she wrote to Virginia, found that 'my past arose and looked me in the face' in the person of Violet Trefusis, fleeing the Continent where she had been living and 'rather pathetic … so forlorn – with her house and all her possessions gone'. Vita had been wary of a meeting, writing to Violet that the love they had always had for one another was 'an unexploded bomb'. She did not want to fall in love with Violet all over again.

Virginia responded that she remembered Violet 'like a fox cub, all scent and seduction'. But in that dark winter, a flooded River Ouse left Rodmell marooned. At Monk's House, Virginia was cut off from the London world which had meant so much to her. At the end of January she was battling depression, as her diary reveals. 'This trough of despair shall not, I swear, engulf me. The solitude is great. Rodmell life is very small beer. The house is damp. The house is untidy. But there is no alternative. What I need is the old spurt.' Vita went to visit Rodmell again on 17 February, taking a firelighter as a gift. They exchanged a few more letters – about hay, in desperately short supply, to feed cattle – and about the likely starvation of Vita's budgerigars.

Finishing *Between the Acts*, Virginia felt she no longer knew for whom she was writing – felt, she said, 'no echo in Rodmell – only waste air'. Describing a local pageant in the grounds of a great country house – a pageant telling the history of an England now threatened by Fascism – the book could be seen as the kind of reverse side of a coin to *Orlando*. It has been described by one critic as the longest suicide note in history – and one addressed to Vita.

On 8 March, Virginia's diary still shows her determined. 'Oh dear yes, I shall conquer this mood. It's a question of letting things come one after the other. Now to cook the haddock.' But ten days later she came back from one of her regular walks soaking, saying she had fallen into one of the dykes.

Virginia was suffering from headaches and sleeplessness, refusing to eat. Her hands shaking, she had lost her power over words, convinced this latest novel was no good. On 27 March, Leonard insisted on consulting Dr Octavia Wilberforce, a Brighton-based friend and connection of the family. Virginia begged her not to insist on a rest cure – the medicine of the day – but Dr Wilberforce had nothing else to offer. The next day, 28 March, Virginia took her coat and walking stick and let herself out of the garden gate, walking towards the Ouse. At lunchtime Leonard discovered notes to himself and to Vanessa on the mantelpiece of their first-floor sitting room.

To Leonard, her 'Dearest', Virginia wrote that she felt certain she was going mad again – and that they could not go through another of those terrible times. She was hearing voices, and could not concentrate. She was doing what seemed the best thing to do. Leonard, she assured him, had given her 'the greatest possible happiness. You have been in every way all that anyone could be.' No two people could have been happier 'until this terrible disease came … I owe all the happiness of my life to you.'

The note to Vanessa echoed the same theme: 'I feel that I have gone too far this time to come back again … I have fought against it, but I can't any longer.'

Leonard has been blamed for imposing on Virginia a regime she hated; Dr Wilberforce for dismissing Virginia's attempts to talk about her past, the ghosts she was raising, as 'balderdash'. But Vanessa too urged Virginia in a letter: 'You *must* be sensible, which means you must accept the fact that Leonard and I can judge better than

Virginia often took lengthy walks along the River Ouse, across the water meadows behind Monk's House. She wrote that an empty landscape allowed her mind to swim free. But in the end, the Ouse would be the scene of her suicide.

you … What shall we do when we're invaded if you're a helpless invalid?' Vanessa was grateful, she would say, that Leonard's love had helped her sister survive this long.

Leonard found himself having to write to the press explaining that Virginia had taken her life because she feared she was going mad – it was not that she was was too weak for the war, and could not 'carry on'. Indeed, Virginia had not run away from the fight – taking first-aid classes, sending saucepans to be melted down, adopting the prescribed brace positions as, while they were eating lunch at Monk's House, the first German planes flew overhead. But Leonard's very defensive insistence has perhaps obscured the fact that many people, in these days, were living at close terms with death.

Leonard wrote to Vita on the evening of 28 March, not wanting her to see in the paper or hear on the wireless (as did Adrian Stephen) 'the terrible thing that has happened to Virginia.'

He gave Vita the basic facts – that Virginia had gone out leaving a suicide note; that he thought she had drowned herself, since he found her stick floating in the river. That they had not found the body … Generously, he added: 'I know what you will feel & what you felt for her. She was very fond of you. She has been through hell these last days.'

From Sissinghurst, Vita wrote to Harold: 'I have just had the most awful shock: Virginia has killed herself.'

'I simply can't take it in. That lovely mind, that lovely spirit. And she seemed so well when I last saw her …' Harold came down to be with her that evening, though Virginia's name was not mentioned between them. There was, as Harold acknowledged later, nothing to be said. A few days later he wrote to her: 'My dearest I know that Virginia meant something to you which nobody else can ever meant and that you will feel deprived of a particular sort of haven which was a background comfort and strength.'

Yet Vita's letter to Harold had crossed in the post with one from him expressing his fears about her 'dual personality. The one tender, wise, and with such a sense of responsibility. And the other rather cruel and extravagant …' He would never reproach her directly for her drinking but her state on his last visit – distraught at being forced to put down one of her beloved Alsatians – had caused him real concern.

Vanessa – who had come to Monk's House on the day of Virginia's disappearance – likewise wrote to Vita on 29 March, 'only because I want to be in touch with you somehow, as the person Virginia loved most I think outside her family'. Vita replied on 31 March, grateful that Virginia's sister, like her husband, had thought of her in their distress: 'I know

'The loveliest mind and spirit I ever knew, immortal both to the world and to us who loved her …'

there is nothing I can do so it's no good wishing I could do something – but if I could see you sometimes I should be most grateful. Is this selfish? You will not think so, for you know how I loved her.' And to Leonard: 'The loveliest mind and spirit I ever knew, immortal both to the world and to us who loved her … For you I feel a really overwhelming sorrow, and for myself a loss which can never diminish.'

She told Harold the blank in her life would be irreparable. Many years later she would write to Harold 'I still think that I might have saved her if only I had been there and had known the state of mind she was getting into.' But perhaps that is a common fallacy. On 8 April she went to visit Vanessa, and Leonard at Rodmell,

Stephen Tomlin's 1931 bust of Virginia. She complained that sitting for him on six afternoons made her feel 'like a piece of whalebone bent'.

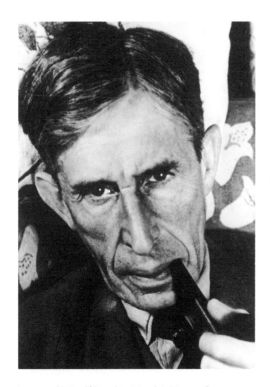

Leonard Woolf lived in Monk's House for many years after Virginia's death, and a bronze bust of him now stands near hers in the garden.

finding Virginia's needlework still lying on a chair.

Virginia's body was not found until 18 April, lodged in a bend in the river. Vita was horrified – she had 'felt there was something fitting in the idea of her being carried out to sea'. But she was glad Virginia's body had been cremated (in Brighton, with Leonard there). 'It is such a clean fiery way … How much I prefer the flames to the worms.'

Leonard buried Virginia's ashes at the foot of one of the great elm trees in the garden of Monk's House – 'two great elms there with boughs interlaced which we always called Leonard and Virginia.' (In January 1943, in a great gale, one of them blew down; the other too has since been lost.)

When the first news came of Virginia's death, Vita told Harold she was afraid he would commit suicide too. 'I do not see him living without her.' These fears were unfounded, however. Leonard's first task was to complete the editing of, and see through to publication, Virginia's *Between the Acts*. He would continue himself to write and to broadcast but he was also of course the keeper of Virginia's literary estate, and in the years ahead would bring out a long series of her essays, stories and diaries, and answer endless queries from a mounting tide of scholars about her life and opinions. On a personal level, however, he was from 1943 close to the South African-born artist Trekkie Parsons (happily married to the chairman of Chatto & Windus), who would be his friend and neighbour, in London and at Monk's House, until his death.

He would remain always on friendly terms also with the Nicolsons, despite professional disagreements. Just a year after Virginia's death, at the urging of his business partner John Lehmann, he agreed to reject Vita's novel *Grand Canyon*, a bizarre tale about Hitler. 'My mind reels before Vita and the universe', he sighed. She never published with the Hogarth Press again. (In 1946 it would in any case be incorporated into Chatto & Windus.)

Leonard wrote later in his memoirs that it was characteristic of Vita that she was 'not in the least bit hurt or resentful and the whole thing made no difference to her relationship with us'. She had always, he said, been the publisher's ideal author. But the fact was the chief link between the Woolfs and the Nicolsons was gone. T.S. Eliot had put his finger on it. Virginia, he said, had been 'a kind of pin which held a lot of people together … these people would now become separate individuals.' It was perhaps the last of Bloomsbury – though like Virginia herself it would be a potent ghost.

CHAPTER 8

⋮ 1943–62 ⋮

In the July after Virginia's death Harold Nicolson was fired from his post in the wartime coalition government – not for any failure as such, but perhaps because ultimately, as his son Nigel put it, he 'was considered dispensable because he was not formidable'. He was still of course an MP, as well as a Governor of the BBC and an unofficial diplomat, encouraged to maintain links with de Gaulle and the Free French. But he felt like a 'might-have-been'.

Six months after Virginia's death Vita's diary too was full of painful entries. 'Alone here. A sudden longing for Virginia. Not much good.' With Harold's return, and with her conception at the start of 1943 of a book about the two St Theresas, *The Eagle and the Dove*, she had brightened to a degree.

But as the war bit ever deeper, and prospects looked ever worse, the Nicolsons were saddened by the political climate and the growth in government circles of anti-Churchill feeling. Their sons were leaving for military service overseas. In February 1944 Knole was bombed and the blast broke windows all round the house, including the one in Vita's old bedroom, and Vita 'broke down completely'. Harold told his diary, 'the whole incident opens a sad wound'. She wrote to him that she always thought she had finally torn Knole out of her heart 'and then the moment anything touches it every nerve is is alive again'. Ethel Smyth died in May; in July Rosamund Grosvenor was killed when a bomb fell on the Savoy Chapel.

Life at Sissinghurst, Vita said, was 'like sleeping in the Piccadilly Underground'. Harold wrote to their sons that they were dominated by aeroplanes. 'All night they howl and rage above us.' At the end of that year Vita wrote to him that she had been down to the lake but had lost all pleasure in it, and in the bluebell woods she had once described as 'a dream', since the soldiers 'invaded them'. She never expected to feel the same way about them again. Pain in her back – long a concern – was making it difficult to garden; 'I feel that I and the lake and the woods are all damaged and spoilt forever.'

Not even Vita's beloved Knole was immune from damage during the war years.

Vita wrote that gardening was largely a question of mixing different sorts of plants 'and seeing how they marry happily together'.

In that winter of 1944–45 Harold wrote to her that, for people like them, the world was becoming a grim place. She for her part wrote that she hated democracy, hated '*la populace*', wished education had never been invented … Many of their class, frightened of the shape the post-war world looked like taking, felt the same way. The last months of the war were coming, but the election in July saw Harold lose his seat – despite the fact that Vita had altered the habits of a lifetime to support his campaign. He would be sent as part of the British delegation to the Nuremberg trials – and in 1948 would try and fail to get into Parliament again – but his life was settling into a more private sphere in which Sissinghurst was key.

After Christmas 1946 he told his diary: 'In the afternoon I moon about with Vita trying to convince her that planning is an element in gardening. She wishes just to jab in the things which she has left over …' If his was the planning – Vita's the planting – then for both there was work to be done. The garden had been wrecked by the war and now, even as their staff returned to them, it had to be recreated on different, more labour-saving, lines. Lawns had to be ploughed up and re-seeded, weeds and elder dug out.

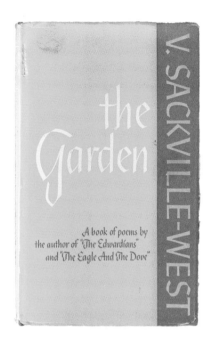

Vita's poem *The Garden* reflected not only her delight in natural beauty, but the darkness of the war years.

A couple of years later Harold wrote that 'Sissinghurst has a quality of mellowness, of retirement, of unflaunting dignity which is just what we wanted to achieve and in some ways have achieved by chance.' It was, he decided, due to the 'succession of privacies' – and thinking of its layout, it is hard to disagree. 'A series of escapes from the world giving a progression of cumulative escape.'

At the end of 1947 Vita was made a Companion of Honour for her services to literature. (Virginia had turned down the same honour, years before.) Vita said she had given up writing for gardening, but in fact her long poem *The Garden*, though she feared it out of touch, was followed by a book about Louis XIV's cousin, *La Grande Mademoiselle*. When *The Garden* won the Heinemann Prize, she spent all the money on azaleas for the moat walk at Sissinghurst, where in spring the rosy blossom can still be seen today.

She began a long-running weekly column in *The Observer* called 'In Your Garden'. Her style was idiosyncratic, assuring the reader who accused her of being an armchair gardener that 'for the last forty years of my life I have broken my back, my finger-nails, and sometimes my heart, in the practical pursuit of my favourite occupation'.

She wrote that she abhorred fanciful description, yet she was the mistress of the memorable phrase: pansies with their 'queer cat-faces of crumpled velvet', in such a variety of colours the ground should appear 'as though spread with the most sumptuous carpet from Isfahan'. One August she could write of the high summer nights when everything was breathless and she would sit and gaze amid the sounds of 'the young owls hissing in their nest over the cowshed, the bray of a donkey, the plop of an acorn into the pool'.

The next year she became a member of the National Trust's Gardens Committee, and thus involved in the acquisition of some of its most notable garden properties, including Hidcote and Winkworth Arboretum. Her attitude to the Trust was ambivalent. In the chill days after the war, when every great house was in trouble, it was agreed that Knole should eventually pass to the Trust, with the proviso that Lord Sackville and his heirs would continue to live in part of the property. She accepted the task of writing the first guide book, and set about it 'quite coldly and unmovedly', only to find the loss biting down on her 'like rodent teeth closing'. 'Knole, which I love more than anything else in the world except Hadji … Knole which has been given to someone else and not to us.'

In her last summer, however, more than a decade on, she visited Knole several times and was pleased to find it looking 'lovelier than ever'. 'I deeply respect and admire the National Trust and all that it does for the salvation of properties,' she had written. 'I don't know where we should be without it.' But emotionally, she could not help regarding it as 'a betrayal of all the tradition of my ancestors and the house I loved.'

She could not understand herself why 'stones and roofs and shapes of courtyards' should matter so poignantly to her. But they did, perhaps, as Harold reassured her, because to her Knole was 'far more a person than a house'. Her distress continued: on another occasion she apologised to him for having wept about it in his room, for the hysteria it provoked in her. 'Knole is mine and I am Knole's and that is that.'

Harold himself was receiving accolades for his writing – in 1948 he was asked to write the official life of George V, a task which involved a good deal of time spent in the royal archives at Windsor. Vita continued to dig herself in down at Sissinghurst. James Lees-Milne (whose wife Avilde was one of Vita's lovers) described her in the early 1950s as having a mixture of grandeur and gypsy qualities which a younger Vita might have recognised.

Totally indifferent to her appearance yet immensely distinguished, she stood tall and upright with her straight nose, 'melancholy mouth' and deep, sad brown eyes. He noted in detail her usual dress of plain blouse with an open neck and single string of pearls. She wore drop earrings. Vita was seldom seen in a skirt, preferring breeches laced below the knee, and high laced boots, 'into the left one of which a pair of secateurs was stuck.'

The 1953 New Year's Honours list brought a knighthood for Harold, though he had been disappointed in his hopes of a peerage that would give him a voice in public affairs, and Vita disliked being addressed as Lady Nicolson even less than she had Mrs Nicolson. The year also brought the marriage of their son Nigel, who had himself the year before become an MP, as well as co-founder of the publishing house Weidenfeld & Nicolson.

Vita and Harold were aware of getting older and both loathed the fact, less for getting 'fat and bald and what-have-you' but because they so loved, and so hated the thought of leaving, 'Life'. Life – and Sissinghurst. As Harold wrote to Vita: 'The garden today is a thing of exceptional merit; but we must make it one of the loveliest in all England.' It was a great work upon which they were engaged, 'and a solace for our senility.' Touchingly, in her sixties and already creator of a widely famous garden, Vita began to take a correspondence course in horticulture, uncomfortably aware still of her amateur status.

But Sissinghurst's future was now an issue. In her diary on 29 November 1954, Vita recorded that Nigel had been sounding Harold out on the question of her ever giving Sissinghurst to the National Trust. 'I said, Never, never, never! *Au grand jamais, jamais.* Never, never, never! Not that hard little metal plate at my door!' Nigel could do what he liked when she was dead, but so long as she lived, no one was going to take 'my darling. It is bad enough to have lost my Knole, but they shan't take Sissinghurst from me.'

In March 1955 Harold had a stroke, which left Vita wondering 'how I could most tidily dispose of myself if he died, as I should not care to go on living without him.' He recovered, but had a second small stroke in May, and was told to take things more easily. Vita too now had arthritis in her hands as well as her back, making it difficult for her to write as well as to garden. Once, she fell down the steep Tower stairs.

When Vita and Harold set off on a cruise in January 1962 Vita seemed unwell, but reassured Harold it was only bronchitis and lumbago; in fact, she was concealing a haemorrhage, caused by abdominal cancer. When they got home, their two diaries reveal their anxieties for each other. Harold, terrified, was heartened after Vita's operation by a Grenadier in full uniform who appeared at the door bearing a message of sympathy from the Queen. 'This is not a nice patch for us to be going through', Vita wrote to him from hospital, but these 'bothers' happened as one got older, and she was determined not to be more of a 'bore and a worry' than she could help – hoped, indeed, soon to be home 'all gay and happy again'.

But Vita failed to recover her strength, and Harold was told to prepare for the worst. Vita had been moved to Priest's House at Sissinghurst for easier nursing; by May it was in a wheelchair that she travelled across the White Garden, across the Tower lawn, to see the spring garden in the last gasp of its seasonal glory, through the Nuttery and back up the moat walk.

On 2 June 1962, a lovely morning, Harold rose early and walked around the garden. Vita died at lunchtime 'without fear or self-reproach'. He went around the garden picking some of her favourite flowers to lay on the bed. The funeral was held at Sissinghurst church, but her ashes would be placed in the Sackville family crypt at Withyham.

Six months after Vita's death Harold was still 'horribly unhappy'. His son remembers him weeping, quietly at the dinner-table and noisily in the far reaches of the garden. On 1 May 1968 Harold died of a heart attack, while undressing for bed.

Leonard Woolf too died some fourteen months later, some time after suffering what may also have been a stroke. One of his last pleasures was listening to Quentin Bell – Virginia's nephew and the biographer that Leonard had chosen for her – read passages from the draft of his book about her. Leonard's ashes were buried under that surviving elm. But he will forever be remembered as the keeper of Virginia's flame.

Opposite: Photographed at Sissinghurst in their last years, Vita and Harold were as united as ever – though the contrast in their costumes shows the different paths their careers had taken. Following pages: The White Garden at Sissinghurst is perhaps the most famous of Vita and Harold's creations. She was intrigued by the idea of a one-colour garden – or rather, of a grey, green, white and silver garden 'which looks so cool on a summer evening'.

Afterlife

It is more than 75 years since Virginia Woolf's death, and those years have seen many different Virginias in the public eye. From the feminist icon to the frail, fey spirit too refined for the real world; from the madwoman to one of the foremost modernist writers of the twentieth century. She herself often contemplated the difficulty of biography, of attempting to show anything but one single side of a subject's identity, and the Virginia whom Vita knew, who sat with her in the firelight of a Bloomsbury flat ruffling Vita's hair, who delighted in exchanging risqué banter with her, has perhaps been lost to our view.

At the time she died, some thought her out of touch with the harsh realities of the world, and it took three decades for that misperception to be overcome. It was in the revolutionary 1960s that a new appraisal really got underway, but we have still some way to go in recognising how revolutionary was her substance as well as

The 2018 film *Vita and Virginia*, starring Gemma Arterton (right) and Elizabeth Debicki.

her style – her vision of an outsider culture, her explorations of gender and identity. In recent decades the volume of her published works has reached extraordinary proportions, comprising as it does her many letters (edited by Vita's son Nigel, who also edited his father's diaries), articles, essays and reviews, polemical writings and biography as well as the novels.

She has made regular appearances in culture high and low, from 1962 when Edward Albee's play, and subsequent Burton/Taylor film, *Who's Afraid of Virginia Woolf?* first substituted her name for that of the 'big bad' wolf. *To the Lighthouse* was filmed in 1983, *Orlando* in 1992, with Tilda Swinton memorably cast in the title role. Five years later Vanessa Redgrave took the lead in *Mrs Dalloway*; five years after that Nicole Kidman in a prosthetic nose played Virginia Woolf herself in *The Hours*, which also starred Meryl Streep and Julianne Moore as other women whose stories relate to *Mrs Dalloway*. Songs and ballet have likewise been inspired by her.

Vita's afterlife is at once simpler and more complex. Simpler, in that she presents fewer different faces to the gaze. More complex, in that the legacy for which she is best remembered is by its nature in a state of constant flux. Each year the seasonal pattern of Sissinghurst – the garden's growth and dying away – poses a series of questions for those who care for it. Each piece of pruning or planting poses the challenge of simultaneously preserving Vita's garden as she left it, and of preserving in it the spirit of her own innovation and adventure.

Richard Burton and Elizabeth Taylor play the warring couple in *Who's Afraid of Virginia Woolf?*

Vita herself never regarded the garden as a finished work, writing of her plans to plant a slow-growing pink magnolia, careless that the visitors who saw it in maturity might not arrive for another century. She told an early meeting of the National Trust that 'it was all very well for the Trust to reserve the old beauties of England but what about the new beauties? … since it was no good trying to resist change, see whether beauty couldn't be made out of [new] things too.'

In 1954 she wrote to Harold about how strange it was to be classed with Hidcote, and how funny it was 'our rubbish dump has blundered into fame'. Today Sissinghurst welcomes some 200,000 visitors a year.

In a sense her personal reputation, too, would continue to be a work in progress. Though her affair with Violet Trefusis had been 'common gossip' in its day, the decision of her son Nigel Nicolson to publish the chronicle of it he found in that Gladstone bag in Vita's tower was still a controversial one. Now *Portrait of a Marriage* – what he described as 'a document unique in the vast literature of love' – is surely better known than Vita's novels, let alone her poetry, though she (and Virginia) rated the latter more highly.

Almost 30 years ago *Portrait of a Marriage* became a television series, with Janet McTeer cast as Vita. Now, Eileen Atkins' successful play *Vita and Virginia* has itself become a film. Vita hoped that the memoir that became *Portrait*, that memoir she left in that Gladstone bag, might be of help to others who like her rejected the simple binary definition of sexual identity. She believed that 'with the progress of the world' such connections as she had shared with Violet Trefusis 'will to a very large extent cease to be regarded as merely unnatural and will be understood far better'. Her connection with Virginia Woolf, so much longer-lasting, so bolstered as it was by the kindness of all involved – husbands, lovers, relatives, friends – may offer yet more lessons for the twenty-first century.

Vita was passionate about old roses, and liked to think the richly coloured scented *Rosa gallica* she found growing in what is now the Orchard had been there since the sixteenth century. 'If you were born with a romantic nature, all roses must be crammed with romance', she wrote.

Discovering More

Sissinghurst Castle Garden

No one can fail to be swept away by the garden Vita Sackville-West created and the National Trust have looked after and developed down the years. Visitors can see the tower room where Vita wrote, the library and the cottage where she and Harold slept, as well as famous features like the White Garden and the Nuttery. Everyone has their own favourite glimpse of Sissinghurst, whether it's the magical springtime carpet of bulbs along the Lime Walk, the blazing summer colours of the Cottage Garden, or the white pigeons fluttering through the arch of the great Elizabethan barn. A vegetable garden supplies the restaurant and plant shop, while visitors can also walk through 460 acres (186 hectares) of the estate, past the lake to the bluebell woods where stones mark the graves of Vita and Harold's dogs.

· Biddenden Road, near Cranbrook, Kent TN17 2AB

· www.nationaltrust.org.uk/sissinghurst-castle-garden

Knole

Vita's ancestral home still boasts all the splendours she described, with notable paintings and important furniture. An ongoing massive restoration project has closed some of the rooms but returned others to their original glory, while giving visitors a chance to see the conservators' work in progress. Climb the Gatehouse Tower to admire the view, and the deer that roam the park.

· Sevenoaks, Kent TN15 0RP (Satnav TN13 1HU)

· www.nationaltrust.org.uk/knole

Virginia's writing room at Monk's House.

Monk's House

The small brick and weatherboard writer's retreat Virginia and Leonard shared is only a few miles outside Lewes, but feels impressively remote, lost down a winding country lane. The ground floor is still as they knew it, with the walls painted in the colours Virginia chose, an evocative scattering of books and papers, and an eclectic mixture of furnishings, from the painted table and chairs created for Virginia by Vanessa Bell and Duncan Grant to the kitchen equipment with which she would bake bread. Across the garden, the room where Virginia wrote so many books, with its formal flower beds and vegetable patch, its greenhouses and lawns, looks out over the South Downs.

· Rodmell, Lewes, East Sussex BN7 3HF

· www.nationaltrust.org.uk/monks-house

Charleston

At Vanessa Bell's home of Charleston, the colourful rooms were themselves the canvases of the artists who lived and worked there, many of whose works also hang on the walls. Owned by a private trust, with shop and tearoom, it is open to the public on a regular basis, but tours to view the house itself must be booked in advance.

· Firle, Lewes, East Sussex BN8 6LL

· charleston.org.uk

Bloomsbury, London

No understanding of Virginia Woolf can be complete without a walk around the district that gave her coterie its name. The house in Tavistock Square where the Woolfs lived for so long was destroyed in the war, and is now part of the Tavistock Hotel, whose bar-cum-pub is named the 'Woolf and Whistle'! But blue plaques mark other houses where the 'Bloomsberries' lived, though many of them are now offices, or absorbed into the nearby university. (A blue plaque also marks Vita's house in the very different surroundings of Belgravia's Ebury Street.) There are memorials to the Bloomsbury set in several of the squares, but it is the topography itself, the very closeness of one 'Bloomsberry' dwelling to another, that gives a real glimpse into the group.

Also:

Smallhythe Place, Tenterden, Kent

The beautiful half-timbered building, now looked after by the National Trust, was home to the great actress Ellen Terry, whose daughter Edy made it a shrine to her memory. Edy and the two women with whom she lived were affectionately known to Vita as 'the trouts'.

· Smallhythe, Tenterden, Kent TN30 7NG
· www.nationaltrust.org.uk/smallhythe-place

Long Barn, Sevenoaks, Kent

Vita and Harold's first home is still a private dwelling, but the gardens are occasionally open for charity.

Cambridge

Trinity College educated many of the Bloomsbury set, and it was lecturing at the less glamorous women's colleges of Girton and Newnham that gave Virginia the impetus to write *A Room of One's Own*. The Orchard tea rooms at Grantchester hosted a young Virginia in company with Rupert Brooke and many future 'Bloomsberries'.

St Ives, Cornwall

The Cornish town where the Stephen family spent so many summers is now better known for its Tate gallery and Barbara Hepworth museum, but there is much the Stephens would recognise about the beach and working harbour while their home, Talland House, is now available as holiday accommodation.

The London parks and waterways

Virginia Woolf was particularly fond of London's green spaces. As a child she often visited Kensington Gardens; she set a story in Kew Gardens; took a jaunt to Hampstead Heath. Regent's Park was the site of many of the walks that helped her compose phrases, while the London Zoo was the site of outings with Vita. Mrs Dalloway walks across St James' Park, with its 'slow-swimming happy ducks', to Piccadilly and Hatchards bookshop, another place Virginia would recognise today. As one who loved London's history Virginia also had a particular feeling for the Thames and its environs. In the first days of their marriage she and Leonard ate their meals at the still-extant Cock Tavern, between Fleet Street and the river.

Selected further reading

Biographical and critical studies on Vita Sackville-West and, in particular, Virginia Woolf and the Bloomsbury group, are as plentiful as leaves on the trees. I therefore chose – both in writing this book, and in suggesting any further reading – to prioritise works by the two women themselves or by their families, with only a very few of the most notable recent biographies.

That was, after all, no great hardship, since their circle was quite staggeringly prolific. Vita not only included a strong autobiographical element in many of her writings but would be written of by her son Nigel (who also edited his father Harold's diaries and letters) and by several of her grandchildren; to say nothing of Violet Trefusis. Virginia's first great biographer was her nephew Quentin Bell; her diaries and letters have been published in numerous volumes; while Leonard Woolf also left several volumes of his own memoirs. But among so many, a baker's dozen of books for the general reader might include:

Dennison, Matthew, *Behind the Mask: The Life of Vita Sackville-West*, William Collins 2014

Glendinning, Victoria, *Vita: The Life of Vita Sackville-West*, Weidenfeld & Nicolson 1973

Gordon, Lyndall, *Virginia Woolf: A Writer's Life* (revised edition), Virago 2006

Lee, Hermione, *Virginia Woolf*, Chatto & Windus 1996

Nicolson, Juliet, *A House Full of Daughters*, Chatto & Windus 2016

Nicolson, Nigel, *Portrait of a Marriage*, Weidenfeld & Nicolson 1973

Nicolson, Nigel (ed.), *Vita & Harold: The Letters of Vita Sackville-West & Harold Nicolson 1910–1962*, Weidenfeld & Nicolson 1992

Sackville-West, Vita, Louise DeSalvo & Mitchell Leaska (ed.), *The Letters of Vita Sackville-West to Virginia Woolf*, Hutchinson 1984

Sackville-West, Vita and Raven, Sarah, *Sissinghurst: The Creation of a Garden*, Virago 2014

Sackville-West, Vita, *Knole and the Sackvilles*, National Trust 1991

Woolf, Virginia, *Illustrated Letters*, selected and introduced by Frances Spalding, National Trust 2017

Woolf, Virginia, *A Room of One's Own*. Like *Orlando*, *Mrs Dalloway* and *To the Lighthouse* it is available in many editions.

Woolf, Virginia, *Selected Diaries*, Vintage 2008

Acknowledgements

As a writer, anyone who dares to contemplate publishing on either Virginia Woolf or Vita Sackville-West is obviously standing on the shoulders of giants – the many writers who have gone before. Closer to the ground, however, I owe a debt to many of the staff and volunteers at the relevant National Trust houses, among whom I would like particularly to thank Vicky McBrien at Sissinghurst, Helen Fawbert at Knole, and Allison Pritchard at Monk's House, as well as Katie Bond, Amy Feldman and Claire Masset in the NT publishing team. Like every other biographer, I am enormously grateful to the staff of the London Library – and grateful also to Nicola Newman and Peter Taylor at Pavilion Books. I also, as always, owe a most heartfelt 'thank you' to Margaret Gaskin, who did so much to help me polish this text.

Picture credits

4, 137 © National Trust Images/Jonathan Buckley; 6, 80, 82 REX/Shutterstock; 7, 8–9, 115, 118–119, 122, 123, 156, 162–163, 167 © National Trust Images/Andrew Butler; 10, 11, 14, 24, 64, 104 (top, bottom left and bottom right), 112, 121, 157 © National Trust Images/John Hammond; 12–13, 78–79, 124–125 Stripey Leaf © Cressida Bell; 15 © National Trust Images/Horst Kolo; 16 © National Trust Images/Jo Hatcher; 17, 107, 161 National Trust; 19 © National Trust /Brian Tremain; 20, 23, 126 © National Trust/ Anthony Lambert; 22 © National Trust Images; 25 (left), 72–73, 142–143, 149 © National Trust Images/James Dobson; 25 (right) © National Trust Images/Derrick E. Witty; 27, 56 Wikimedia Commons; 28 Art Collection 2/Alamy Stock Photo; 30 MS Thr 557 (179), Houghton Library, Harvard University; 31 Universal Art Archive/Alamy Stock Photo; 32 Royal Photographic Society/Getty Images; 33, 42 Granger Historical Picture Archive/Alamy Stock Photo; 34 MS Thr 557 (93), Houghton Library, Harvard University; 35, 45, 98 Paul Fearn/Alamy Stock Photo; 36 George C Beresford/Getty Images; 39 MS Thr 557 (184), Houghton Library, Harvard University; 40 Richard Donovan/Alamy Stock Photo; 47, 109 Culture Club/Getty Images; 52 Invitation for the Omega Workshop (w/c on paper), Fry, Roger Eliot (1866–1934) / Private Collection / Photo © Peter Nahum at The Leicester Galleries, London / Bridgeman Images; 55 © National Trust /Amy Law; 57 MS Thr 560 (138), Houghton Library, Harvard University; 58 Luise Berg-Ehlers/ Alamy Stock Photo; 60, 89 Sasha/Getty Images; 61 Angelo Hornak/Alamy Stock Photo; 62 MS Thr 557 (201), Houghton Library, Harvard University; 63 Universal Images Group/Getty Images; 65, 75, 76 © National Trust Images/Caroline Arber; 71 Jeff Overs/ Getty Images; 74, 92–93, 141, 168 © National Trust Images/Andreas von Einsiedel; 77 Elizabeth Whiting & Associates/Alamy Stock Photo; 83 MS Thr 560 (100), Houghton Library, Harvard University; 85, 130 © Estate of Vanessa Bell, courtesy Henrietta Garnett; 87 MS Thr 564 (92), Houghton Library, Harvard University; 90 © National Trust/ Charles Thomas; 91 MS Thr 564 (93), Houghton Library, Harvard University; 101 Moviestore Collection Ltd/Alamy Stock Photo; 102, 138, 155 © National Trust Images/David Sellman; 105, 164 Pictorial Press Ltd/Alamy Stock Photo; 111 MS Thr 560 (145), Houghton Library, Harvard University; 116 © National Trust Images/Andrew Lawson; 128 MS Thr 560 (93), Houghton Library, Harvard University; 133 MS Thr 562 (43), Houghton Library, Harvard University; 134 INTERFOTO/Alamy Stock Photo; 144 Eric Harlow/Keystone/Getty Images; 145 MS Thr 561 (48), Houghton Library, Harvard University; 146 MS Thr 560 (5), Houghton Library, Harvard University; 151 © National Trust Images/Eric Crichton; 152 Chronicle/Alamy Stock Photo; 165 ScreenProd/Photononstop/Alamy Stock Photo

Cover images: Vita Sackville-West: E.O. Hoppe/Getty Images; Virginia Woolf: Granger Historical Picture Archive/Alamy Stock Photo

Index